WHEN ALL
Hell
BREAKS LOOSE

WHEN ALL
Hell
BREAKS LOOSE

How to Move Forward When Life Sets You Back

DEBORAH WITTMIER

XULON PRESS

Xulon Press
2301 Lucien Way #415
Maitland, FL 32751
407.339.4217
www.xulonpress.com

When All Hell Breaks Loose:
How to Move Forward When Life Sets You Back
© 2021 by Deborah Wittmier

All emphasis is the author's own.

Paperback ISBN-13: 978-1-6628-2852-2
Hard Cover ISBN-13: 978-1-6628-2853-9
eBook ISBN-13: 978-1-6628-2854-6

To Harvey, whose immeasurable love sweetly reflects that of our Savior, and to the people of Crossfire Church, who stood with us, prayed us through, and listened to many, many messages about adversity—how I love you!

TABLE OF CONTENTS

———

INTRODUCTION

Though I walk through the valley of the shadow of death, I will fear no evil: for thou art with me.
—Psalms 23:4 KJV

O f all the things we hope to avoid, resist, or remove, adversity tops the list. We feel strongly about it, and with good reason. Adversity has a way of sneaking up and exacting costs we do not expect or want to pay. It knows just how to turn life upside down and make the sanest among us wonder who we are. Our reactions to adversity are so visceral that even before we fully understand the matter, we try to muster some semblance of control and end the struggle, one way or another.

Although we seem hardwired to flee adversity, we eventually come to grips with trouble. We adjust to the changes we never asked for, and we manage to find hints of some greater meaning in our mess. Then, if we dig a little deeper, we find unexpected treasures that come only through times of difficulty. With God's help, we can embrace these insights and opportunities and discover something more astounding than the trouble itself (Isa. 61:3).

THE START OF AN UNEXPECTED JOURNEY

To find the goodness hidden within your struggles, you will need to stand against forces that you cannot see. Death, the ultimate enemy, is not limited to the death of the body. It comes in many forms, including loss, destruction, sickness, hopelessness, and strife. Always, death attempts to steal the life and goodness that come from God alone. Resisting this enemy is crucial, because he only has free rein if you grant it.

Not so long ago, death came calling at my house. My husband Harvey and I are local pastors, and we serve other pastors and churches abroad. In May of 2018, we went to Uganda as part of our ongoing work there. Before our trip, I had noticed some changes in my vision. Because of my family history, I scheduled an eye exam, hoping to rule out glaucoma or, at the very least, catch it early. My ophthalmologist gave me a thorough exam, ruled out glaucoma, and arranged for me to have an MRI when Harvey and I returned to the States.

The MRI did its job. It revealed a growth at the base of my pituitary gland—in other words, a brain tumor. Hearing this news set off some alarms, as you might imagine. Harvey and I have been blessed with many years of good health and were now facing the upheaval that millions have faced when an unwelcome diagnosis arrives.

Soon, we consulted a neurosurgeon who had removed more than two thousand such lesions with great success. He explained the MRI findings and said that he would access the tumor without opening my skull. That was a great relief, yet I admit that an instantaneous healing would have been more my cup of tea! I put my preferences aside, however, having learned over time that my will did not always match what God had in mind. His ways of answering my prayers could not be bested, so if His provision for my situation was surgery, then surgery it would be.

Harvey and I had faced our share of crises over the years and knew that prayer and preparation were key. So a week before the surgery, we drove to the mountains for a brief getaway and the perfect place to seek the Lord without distraction. I, for one, needed His insights and wisdom regarding the surgery and anything else He might reveal. Needing His guidance was nothing new, but I personally had no idea how much I needed it *this* time. I only knew what God spoke to my heart: "Though I walk through the valley of the shadow of death, I will fear no evil" (Ps. 23:4 KJV).

The Twenty-third Psalm has always comforted me, but a less soothing side of verse 4 also got my attention. Preachers and commentators describe "the valley of the shadow of death" in various ways, some less discomfiting than others. But there is no escaping the weight of the phrase. I realized that even though my surgery was considered routine, it was far from routine for me. My mind and emotions had to be solidly anchored in truth. So God led me through some intense soul work to weed out any distortions that might trip me up later.

The preparation was intense, yet I could not know everything that lay ahead (1 Cor. 13:9). So I consecrated the entire matter to Jesus' Lordship and rested in His faithfulness. By the time our getaway ended, and the big day arrived, I felt ready. I knew that my heavenly Father had prepared me and provided one of the best neurosurgeons in the business. And I knew that, in the realm of brain operations, this one was fairly easy.

It proved to be anything but. The next forty-eight hours were nothing short of breathtaking, and life going forward was going to look very different from anything I had expected.

PART I

Face to Face
with Adversity

1

GOD PREPARES US

The temptations in your life are no different from what others experience. And God is faithful. He will not allow the temptation to be more than you can stand. When you are tempted, he will show you a way out so that you can endure.

— *1 Corinthians 10:13*

Within hours of entering the hospital, my "routine" procedure turned radical. Instead of one operation, I had four within a forty-eight-hour period. My loved ones watched in horror as hospital personnel repeatedly rushed me out of my room and back to the operating room to address medical emergencies. The fight to save my life was on, and after the fourth operation, I still wasn't out of the woods. A drug-resistant strain of pneumonia had set in and greatly compromised my lungs. The breathing tube that would have come out during a normal recovery stayed in much longer than expected.

For me, those first two days were a blur of procedures and fluctuating states of consciousness. Yet at some point (I believe during the third surgery), I saw the true nature of my struggle. It happened around the time doctors worked to reinsert my breathing tube. Apparently, previous insertions and removals of the tube had caused inflammation. From what I am told, I had difficulty breathing and fought the doctors as they tried to get the tube back in place.

What I saw during that surgery was the battle that raged in two very real worlds. In the temporal, physical realm, I was now strapped to my bed, unable to interfere with the medical equipment that was attached to my body. The scene was intense, but the people around me were working to help me. The scenario in the spirit realm was quite different and revolting. There I saw myself in a dark and desolate junkyard, a place of ruined, worthless things where a large pack of dogs salivated, as though sizing me up for their next meal.

Two things seemed clear: the dogs represented death, and my life hung in the balance. Whether I could or would survive was an open question and had been since my week in the mountains. The junkyard was not a random location. It was the valley of the shadow of death, which Jesus had brought to my attention before my first surgery. Immediately, I realized the gravity of my situation and knew that only Jesus was my help. My medical team was part of His provision for me, but even their diligence would not determine my ultimate outcome. There were much more consequential matters in play.

> My enemies surround me like a pack of dogs; an evil gang closes in on me (Psalms 22:16).

FACING THE FEAR

During the previous week's retreat, God addressed the issue of fear, the sly fox that tries to capitalize on our adversity. Fear is like a computer code operating in the background but showing up in what we say and do. When we are most vulnerable, fear lunges to the foreground and tries to take us down. A brain tumor diagnosis is a perfect setup for fear's exploitation. Whether my surgery was considered routine or not, dealing with fear was a must.

Psalm 23 was part of God's dealing with the issue. It says, "Yea, though I walk through the valley of the shadow of death, I will fear no evil; for You are with me; Your rod and Your staff, they comfort me. You prepare a table before me in the presence of my enemies; You anoint my head with oil; my cup runs over" (Ps. 23:4–5 NKJV). Verse 4 spoke directly to any fear, reminding me to reject it and promising that God would be with me. But it also mentioned the valley of the shadow of death, where danger is possible. Verse 5 was equally paradoxical: it assured me of divine provision but said I would find it *in the presence of my enemies.* The bottom line? God was with me, but I might have to pass through a perilous place, and I needed to prepare for it.

The junkyard scene I saw during surgery was a paradox all its own. Death and his minions were unmistakably present, and they were many. They looked fierce, but I was strangely unafraid of them. My concern was logistical. In my weakened state, getting across the junkyard in one piece would be physically impossible. There was too much distance, and there were too many dogs. My only thought was, "I can't make it across."

Then, suddenly, I felt myself being scooped up from the ground and carried away, the way a bridegroom lifts his bride and carries her across the threshold. It was Jesus! He promised to be with me, and He was! I never saw Him coming; I only knew that He was holding me. As my head hung limp over His arm, I rested and watched the dogs react to His presence. They cringed and shrank back at the sight of Him. Their menacing teeth vanished as they closed their mouths, hunched their shoulders, and lowered their eyes. Not one of those demon spirits dared to look into Jesus' face.

In the next moment, my head flopped the other way and rested against Jesus' chest. I felt the coarseness of His clothing scratching against my cheek. It was not abrasive but comforting. I was in the bosom of my Lord, safe and loved as He carried me across the junkyard with complete authority and not the slightest hesitation. He never looked at the dogs or spoke to them. He simply strode through their midst and finished what He came to do.

Without a word between us, Jesus set me down in safety. Suddenly, I knew Psalm 23 like never before. The Word became flesh in my life! I passed through the valley of the shadow of death, and He was with me. Fear was vanquished, and the open question of whether I would live or die was now closed. *I would not die.* I would fight death with my whole being. Yes, I had already agreed with Jesus that if it was time for me to go home with Him, I would go. But He showed me that it wasn't my time. Therefore, I would stay.

Looking back, I can see that I never had anything to fear—absolutely nothing! The Lord had anointed my head with oil long before my first surgery. Throughout the entire ordeal, my cup ran over with His goodness and mercy, because He was with me. But I had never experienced Him as tangibly and personally as I did in that junkyard. And I never have since.

A Kind of Gethsemane

The soul work done before my first procedure stayed with me then and is with me now. Perhaps I am most amazed that God Himself initiated the experience. This showed me how deeply personal His love is. It also revealed how little rules and regulations mean in our relationship with Him. When He led me into a period of preparation, it was because my well-being mattered to Him.

Looking back, it was a Gethsemane-like experience. The magnitude could not be compared with what Jesus faced (not even close). But there was a parallel: I had to decide whether I would pursue my will or accept the Father's will for me. This was not about a theoretical acceptance but a conscious, intentional setting aside of my preferences, including my preference for a bloodless, instant healing. It would have been fine with me to skip the extreme testing of my faith. Yet I could not condition my faith on any promise of an easy outcome. My trust had to be in the One who understood all things and would see me through, whatever happened.

Settling the trust issue was critical because adversity is disruptive. I don't know anyone who likes disruption. I sure don't. We humans have expectations about how life "ought" to work. So when things get messy, we assume that something is wrong. Sometimes, however, our expectations are off. Whether wittingly or not, we turn our preferences into inner laws that color how we see the world. Unless we expose these beliefs to the light of truth, they become strongholds that govern our choices.

So, for example, if you believe that divine healing is, by definition, instantaneous and should never involve medical intervention, you might see the surgical removal of a brain tumor as being contrary to God's plan. You might even see it as a failure of faith. If you had received my diagnosis, you might have rejected the surgeon's counsel out of hand. Of course, there is nothing wrong with believing that God can heal you in a moment. I believe that He can and often does heal people that way. But, if you insist that He *must* heal you that way, there is a stronghold at work.

Everyone has strongholds of some kind. Over time, our words and actions reveal them. Maybe you habitually avoid confrontation. Perhaps you have internalized the suggestion to "let sleeping dogs lie." Is it ever good advice? Yes. There are moments when even healthy confrontation is counterproductive. But is it wise to avoid confrontation at all times and all costs? I would say not. Habitual avoidance of confrontation is akin to burying your head in the sand. *It is a stronghold.*

Do you harbor such fears? Let God free you! You'll have to face what intimidates you, but you won't face it alone. He will walk you through it. Part of my preparation for brain surgery was to walk through "what if" scenarios. Instead of patting my head and saying, "Don't worry, Deborah. Everything's going to be just fine," the Lord challenged me to decide how I would respond if something went wrong. I confess that "what ifs" are not a brain-tumor patient's favorite subject. But I needed to go there, and in taking me there, the Lord both freed and equipped me. If there was any chance that death would challenge me (and there was), I needed to have my answer in mind before he showed up. That gave me an edge. I didn't have to figure out where I stood when all hell broke loose.

Nobody expected the complications I experienced. There was plenty of shock and surprise to go around. But I was not unprepared, and neither fear nor despair overcame me. I'm no spiritual superhero. I'm simply testifying to God's gracious preparation of my soul. Physically, I was drained and even debilitated. I did not look or feel "put together," and I drifted in and out of consciousness. Yet His preparation equipped me with confidence and assurance—not in anything I could do but in what He had already done. Instead of feeling adrift in a treacherous place, I was secure in His capable hands. God had anchored me in His truth and determined my outcome in advance. My part was to keep agreeing with His plan, whatever shape it took.

Prepared for a Miracle

I'm in awe of how God deals with us. He knows our quirks and helps us to overcome our most formidable obstacle: ourselves. So when He shines His light on one of my "sacred cows" (what I think is right, or how I think things should be), I resist the urge to cover it up. I eventually figured out that when He meddles in my business, He's not out to embarrass me; He's out to *empower* me.

That is exactly what He did in 2018. He helped me to see where my help would come from if my medical situation went sideways. "But," you ask, "didn't you know that already?"

Yes, I've known it for a very long time. But each crisis makes its own demands. I'd never had or needed a neurosurgeon before 2018. Now that I had one, I placed a certain amount of trust in his judgment and skill. After all, he was about to poke around my brain and fix whatever was broken. I needed to trust him, but *within limits*. My medical team was responsible for my medical care, and I valued their expertise. But my life was not in their hands. It was in God's hands. Death was a possibility. I knew that because Jesus and I had talked about it. But I also knew that my death would be His decision and nobody else's. The enemy had no power to choose my death or schedule the date. Nor would my passing result from any kind of medical failure or mishap.

Knowing this was critical to my outcome. However, it did not stop death from pursuing me. My body was taxed to its limits and beyond, more than once. I knew what was happening and recognized the fits of choking, the inability to breathe, and the sense that I was fading away. As far as I was concerned, they were the tools the enemy used in his effort to kill me outright or, at the very least, draw me into agreement with death. If he could convince me to abandon my trust in God, he could take me out. It was that simple.

Much of that time, I was intubated and unable to speak, but I needed to speak. So I kept a pen and notebook on hand and used them to communicate. I still have those notebooks. In one I wrote, "I will not die by a breathing tube. I will not die by choking. I will not die by suffocating." I was standing against death. Breathing tubes are lifesavers, but they have side effects. Mine had been inserted and removed more than once, causing swelling. I'll spare you the nasty details. Suffice to say that my experiences with choking were intense, and I desperately wanted to get off that tube.

My doctors knew how I felt. But they were struggling with their "what ifs": What if they took me off the tube and my lungs failed? What if they couldn't reinsert it? Then what? So when they finally decided to remove it again, there was a stipulation: they would monitor my oxygen levels and see how my lungs did. One young doctor gently prepared me for what seemed to be the inevitable return to intubation. He was obviously distressed about it, so I told him we would simply trust God.

That is what we did. We looked to the One who had given me breath in the first place! I talked to Harvey about two things I needed: I asked for Joe (our son-in-law and our church's worship leader) to sing over me about the breath of God, and I asked for our precious friend Dawn to dance an intercessory dance of life over me. I fully understood my doctors' trepidation, and I knew where my oxygen levels had been. But I also knew that God had already provided everything I needed. We weren't begging for my life; we were partaking of the provision that was already in place.

Both Joe and Dawn honored my requests, and within hours, the young doctor declared that I would not be intubated again! I smiled and reminded him that God was moving in our midst. We rejoiced together, and it was precious. We both knew there was only one explanation for what happened: God had intervened! The enemy who staked out many pathways to my death had patiently waited for me to be offered up. The junkyard dogs licked their chops and anticipated a feast. But Jesus had the last word. He had already provided life, and it swallowed up death. In my need, I experienced His authority firsthand.

"IMMEDIATELY" TAKES TIME

What I just described was a sudden, immediate miracle. One moment my doctor listed all the reasons why the breathing tube would have to be reinserted, and the next moment it was out for good! You have probably had sudden breakthroughs of your own, times when every circumstance said nothing would ever change—and then it did. Scripture is full of such miracles. Some of them involve people whose suffering continued for years or even decades, and then—*poof!*—their suffering was over.

Luke chapter 13 talks about a woman who was physically bent over for eighteen years and then healed in an instant. Imagine walking with your face to the ground, unable to make eye contact with anyone around you, for eighteen years. Then, suddenly, you can stand upright! Luke's account captures the miracle, but apart from the woman's disability, we don't know much about her. The Bible doesn't talk about her pain or about how her condition started. We don't know whether Jesus knew her or had seen her prior to that day. We only know that when He spoke to her and touched her, her suffering ended *immediately*.

Bible accounts don't tell us everything. They tell us what we need to know. Sometimes, the text hints at what happened beforehand, but the details might not be chronological or even in the same book. That is true of when Jesus called Simon Peter and Andrew to follow Him. Here is what Matthew's Gospel tells us:

> *Jesus, walking by the Sea of Galilee, saw two brothers, Simon called Peter, and Andrew his brother, casting a net into the sea; for they were fishermen. Then He said to them, "Follow Me, and I will make you fishers of men." They immediately left their nets and followed Him (Matthew 4:18–20 NKJV).*

"Immediately they left"! Does that amaze you like it does me? Jesus seems to be telling virtual strangers to follow Him, and they do it on the spot. Remember, these men aren't fishing for recreation. Fishing is their business and their livelihood. If they up and quit, they will still have bills to pay. Yet they seem to drop everything, with no questions asked.

Or did they?

We read our Bibles with the benefit of hindsight, so we tend to make certain assumptions. We know that Jesus is the Son of God and His steps are divinely ordained. Therefore, we expect Simon Peter and his brother Andrew to robotically obey Him. We see their meeting as a supernatural event in which earthly questions have no meaning. But is that accurate? Or is hindsight clouding our judgment? Remember that Simon Peter and Andrew were living their lives, not looking forward or backward in history. They didn't know how their story (or Jesus' story) would turn out. Either way, accepting Jesus' invitation was not a foregone conclusion for Jews in their day. Many Jews walked away from Jesus, and some scoffed openly about His claims to be the Son of God.

Simon Peter and Andrew did not reject Him, however. When He said, "Follow Me," they followed Him. Was the outcome of their meeting predetermined? Did some spiritual "magnet" draw them to Jesus and bypass their mental capacity to mull over His request? Is that how God works in people's lives? Do people obey Him because the Holy Spirit makes it impossible for them not to?

Certainly not. There was a backstory, and it reveals God's workings in the brothers' lives. Because the biblical narrative is not necessarily chronological, some details can be scattered in other chapters or books. For example, the four Gospels were written by four men who wrote as they were inspired by the Holy Spirit. Each man recounted Jesus' life and ministry from a particular point of view. None of them told the whole story, but taken together, the four Gospels present a more complete picture of Jesus.

Matthew chapter 4 seems to indicate that Jesus, Simon Peter, and Andrew were meeting for the first time. Matthew never stated as much, but absent any other context, we surmise it. This is why their immediate obedience seems so stunning. But in John's Gospel, we see more of the story. John mentions the three men but provides details that Matthew omits. The key is that those details happened *before* the meeting in Matthew 4 and reveal that the brothers' immediate response was not quite what we thought.

> As Jesus walked by, John looked at him and declared, "Look! There is the Lamb of God!" When John's two disciples heard this, they followed Jesus. Jesus looked around and saw them following. "What do you want?" he asked them. They replied, "Rabbi" (which means "Teacher"), "where are you staying?" "Come and see," he said. It was about four o'clock in the afternoon when they went with him to the place where he was staying, and they remained with him the rest of the day. Andrew, Simon Peter's brother, was one of these men who heard what John said and then followed Jesus. Andrew went to find his brother, Simon, and told him, "We have found the Messiah" (which means "Christ"). Then Andrew brought Simon to meet Jesus. Looking intently at Simon, Jesus said, "Your name is Simon, son of John—but you will be called Cephas" (which means "Peter") (John 1:36–42).

Does the brothers' decision still seem abrupt, or has the backstory explained it? I propose the latter. The apostle John reveals Andrew's hunger for the things of God. When John the Baptist was preaching and baptizing, Andrew was there, as one of his disciples. Then, when John pointed to Jesus and called Him the Lamb of God, Andrew followed Jesus instead. He was so impressed that he told his brother the Messiah was in town! And when Simon Peter first met Jesus, Jesus prophesied over him in a very personal way.

By the time Jesus called the brothers to follow Him, they'd already considered how they would respond. Yes, they dropped everything in a moment, but that moment was the *culmination* of many moments. Jesus had been preparing them for the biggest decision of their lives. The Holy Spirit nurtured in them a hunger for the Messiah and an understanding of their place with Him. They did not come to that moment unequipped or unknowing. Jesus saw to it that they were ready to decide.

I hope the brothers' story gives you hope about the situations and changes for which you are praying. The Holy Spirit is continually preparing you for what is ahead, so you can cooperate with Him. Then, in the fullness of time, your "immediately" will come.

Prepared and Equipped — with Victory

You have probably noticed that your victories come *after* your struggles. God prepares us for both. Jesus told us that we would have tribulation. He also said to be cheerful, because He has overcome the world (John 16:33). In other words, no trouble can outweigh His goodness, mercy, or grace. But being of good cheer does not mean slapping on a happy face and letting the chips fall where they may. It helps to keep smiling, but we are also called to actively participate in the fulfilling of God's will.

That means standing firm, which can cost you something. Why else would God prepare you, and why did He prepare Jesus in the garden of Gethsemane? Jesus did not whistle past the garden and say, "I've got this, Father. Let's move on." He knew He was the Son of God. He knew His part in the plan of salvation. He fully expected to suffer, die, and be buried. He also knew that the Father and the Holy Spirit were with Him and provision for victory had been made. Yet Jesus submitted Himself to a final period of preparation.

In other words, the Son of God humbled Himself. He honestly faced the horror of what was ahead and got down to brass tacks with the Father. His garden experience was excruciating and caused "great drops of blood" to drip from His pores (Luke 22:44 KJV). He was about to undertake something more consequential than any event in history and far more difficult than any human experience. It would transform people's hearts and the creation itself.

Yet Jesus first had to do business with the Father. Neither you nor I can fathom the weight He bore that night. But there are times when God asks us to lay down our wills and ourselves before Him. Theoretically, the choice seems obvious: we will choose God's will. But in reality, the choice is more nuanced. We might even be tempted to skip Gethsemane altogether and just ask God to make sure everything turns out OK.

Friend, your Gethsemane is too important to skip over. Jesus knows that. He has faced the experience, and He will guide you. You don't need to impress Him by acting spiritual. You only need to agree with Him and cooperate with the truth He reveals. Remember: He knows every aspect of your need. He knows your nature. He sees your fears. He is familiar with your weaknesses. He will lead you through every decision, and He will carry you across every junkyard. Your story won't always have a fairy-tale ending. But the One who gave you breath is giving you breath this very moment. And if you cleave to Him, you will remain safe in His care. That is His promise!

My sheep listen to my voice; I know them, and they
follow me. I give them eternal life, and they will never
perish. No one can snatch them away from me, for my

Father has given them to me, and he is more powerful than anyone else. No one can snatch them from the Father's hand (John 10:27–29).

I can testify that God's promise is true. As unexpected and difficult as my brain surgeries were, the episode ended in victory. Death could not snatch me from Jesus' hands! But I did not escape death unscathed. A post-op hemorrhage near the optic nerve left my right eye blinded. I knew from the start that any operation could have unexpected outcomes. Yet the reality of partial blindness surprised me. Every day, I am aware of how much my life has changed. And every day, He helps me to adjust. In all things I continue to praise Him, and He carries me from the dark places, into His light. For that, I am so very grateful.

Live and Learn

Reading books enriches our lives. But combining reading with introspection and application takes learning to an even more fruitful level. You could say that what you read is more likely to "become flesh" when you interact with it. For that reason, each chapter will provide opportunities to interact with what you have read. Answer the questions frankly and the process will answer some of your questions, shedding light on your past and aiding your preparation for your future.

- Which sentence or paragraph in this chapter most resonates with your experience of adversity? What about it spoke directly to you, and what can you take from it going forward?

- Describe the table of provision that God has prepared for you in the presence of your enemies (not human enemies, but difficult circumstances and/or ungodly spiritual forces). How does His provision address your needs at this time? Where does God's provision seem to be lacking or delayed? Might the disparity reflect a difference between His sense of timing and yours? How might your expectations be coloring your perception of His provision?

- Can you remember a time when you skipped your "Gethsemane" experience? Looking back, why might you have skipped it? What might you have gained from it?

2

TAKE MY YOKE

———◆———

*Take my yoke upon you. Let me teach you, because I
am humble and gentle at heart, and you will find rest
for your souls.*

—*Matthew 11:29*

Three months after my first surgery, I sent our ministry partners a second update on my medical situation. The first
sentence read, "Questions, questions, and more questions!" You
can tell it wasn't a rah-rah message, but it wasn't a sob story
either. I simply described the sense that my life had been rearranged and my role was not as clear as it had been in the thick of
the crisis. I shared this knowing that every Christian struggles
with life changes, and what I was learning was for our partners'
benefit as well as mine.

I doubt that my candor surprised anyone. First of all, the
people who receive my letters know me. Secondly, they have
grappled with dichotomies of their own. What I shared about
my confusion had little to do with brain surgery and everything
to do with the yokes we choose. Are we yoked to Jesus the way
He described in Matthew 11:29? Or are we yoked to our own
ideas? My confusion suggested that I entertained the latter.

Where Did the Confusion Start?

I found it strange that recovering was more complicated than dealing with sheer chaos had been. Being home was wonderful, but life was different. Partial blindness left me feeling less sure-footed than before, both physically and in terms of my new role. I became startled when something or somebody moved toward me from my right side. Things popped into my field of vision so suddenly that I often jumped. There was also a question about driving. Harvey and I routinely ran errands together, often stopping for a bite to eat. We loved those times together and still do, but I always had the option to hop in my car and go it alone when I needed to. Suddenly, that choice was off the table.

Despite the obvious adjustments, I was well aware that I had dodged a bullet. So my uneasiness seemed counterintuitive. There had to be a reason for it, but the only clue I had seemed too general, like a very large haystack in which a tiny needle was hidden. The "haystack" was my perspective. I knew that my confusion was tied to my way of seeing my new life. But the "needle" was a mystery.

Before too long, the mystery was solved, and I found what had been hidden: it was a subtle but significant shift in my outlook. During my surgical period, I nestled in the yoke with Jesus, not tugging against Him but cooperating with His movement and pace. It was so obvious that I could not save myself that I never tried to help Him do what only He can do. I had absolutely nothing to contribute, other than to trust Him. Therefore, there was no confusion and no second-guessing my role. I simply leaned into Jesus.

But once the life-and-death issues receded, I tried to climb into the driver's seat with Him. I did it by taking responsibility for my recovery—something I had not done before. Intellectually, I knew that I was powerless to make my body recover, yet buried somewhere in my belief systems was an idea that my sense of logic found very appealing: it was the suggestion that although I most certainly could not perform brain surgery, I was *expected* to "do" recovery.

Do you see how subtle deception is? I had embraced a sense of duty that drew me out of my role and into an area of responsibility that only Jesus could handle. So I slipped out of the yoke and tried to recover as an act of my will. In essence, I tried to share in His Lordship, a choice that never ends well. I did not detect my error because it was operating beneath the level of my conscious awareness. It was a stronghold, and my sense of confusion was the only thing that betrayed its existence. But once I recognized it, I saw how ludicrous it was!

Deception works because it wears disguises. To the natural mind, taking responsibility for my own recovery sounded noble and even godly. But the idea was based in a performance mentality that involves "do-gooding"—the spiritual and emotional quicksand that sucks us into unending cycles of self-improvement. That is futility! We are called to thrive by staying in the yoke with Jesus and trusting Him to form our outcomes. Asking His help in forming our own outcomes is something very, very different.

It is no wonder that my sense of clarity went up in smoke. I had offered God something He never asked for: my performance. He certainly was not impressed by my attempt to play His part! By measuring myself against the size of my problem, I laid the trap that ensnared me. I saw recovery as a project I could manage. But manageability was not the issue; Lordship was. My role was to turn over the entire matter to the One who is Lord.

When I did that, my confusion ended.

Trust in the LORD with all your heart; do not depend on your own understanding. Seek his will in all you do, and he will show you which path to take. Don't be impressed with your own wisdom. Instead, fear the LORD and turn away from evil. Then you will have healing for your body and strength for your bones (Proverbs 3:5–8).

"COME TO ME"

Staying in the yoke with Jesus is a matter of perceiving His Lordship and abiding in Him. The more real His Lordship becomes, the less you want to be your own master. Obviously, He is Lord whether you and I acknowledge it or not. But as we give ourselves to that reality, He becomes increasingly present and reveals more of His goodness through us. Jesus explained it this way:

> *Come to Me, all you who labor and are heavy laden, and I will give you rest. Take My yoke upon you and learn from Me, for I am gentle and lowly in heart, and you will find rest for your souls. For My yoke is easy and My burden is light (Matthew 11:28–30 NKJV).*

Jesus' words are powerfully and prophetically persuasive—enough to make you shout, "Yes, Lord, I want that!" Yet many Christians who know and love this passage still feel weary and over-burdened. Does that mean His promise is empty? Absolutely not! Jesus does not promise what He cannot or will not deliver. Any disconnect is on our end. Perhaps we are reading the passage in a self-focused way, not because we are thoughtless, but because we are heavy-hearted. With the pressures of life bearing down on us, we latch onto His promise to lighten our load, but we gloss over the process He describes.

That process starts when we obey His invitation and *come to Him*. Our burdens don't leave when we hear Jesus' promise. Our burdens become light when we sit in His presence and open ourselves to Him. Doing that means first understanding what "Come to Me" means. Does it mean returning to the church? Coming to the Christian faith? Following Christ? In part, yes, but coming to Jesus is far more personal than that. It is a matter of submitting yourself and becoming intimate with Him.

Think about the way you seek out a trusted friend when something is weighing on your mind. You come fully prepared to bare your soul in a one-on-one exchange. You unburden yourself believing that your friend will listen and even help you. When the conversation is over, your burden seems lighter and easier to carry. The exchange is not transactional; it is relational.

If we are honest, the way we come to Jesus is often less relational than that. We act like children coming home from school with problems crammed into our backpacks. We burst through the front door, call on His name, drop our backpacks on the floor, and get on with whatever is next on our agenda (like running to the fridge or going outside to play). We bring Him our troubles because nothing else is working. We know only He can help us. But we don't linger in His presence. Without realizing it, we bring a drive-thru mentality to the throne room. I am not suggesting that we "try harder" or add superficial spiritual routines to our already overloaded backpacks. Jesus is not after our performance. When He says, "Come to Me," He is simply inviting us to come with our burdens in hand and sit with Him. Then He will make our burdens light.

"I Will Give You Rest"

Do you crave rest? Well, Jesus promised to give it. Why then do so few of us feel rested? I believe the problem is partly in how we define *rest*. For example, Americans equate rest with relaxation, leisure, or any type of break from our responsibilities and the harassment of everyday life. But is that the rest that Jesus promised? Another translation of Matthew 11:28–30 might provide an answer:

> *Are you weary, carrying a heavy burden? Then come to me. I will refresh your life, for I am your oasis. Simply join your life with mine. Learn my ways and you'll discover that I'm gentle, humble, easy to please. You will find refreshment and rest in me. For all that I require of you will be pleasant and easy to bear (Matthew 11:28–30 TPT).*

Look at these words one more time: "I will refresh your life [i.e., give you rest], for *I am your oasis.*" Did you hear that? Jesus is not promising to give you down time, freedom from responsibility, or a trouble-free life. He is promising to *be* your rest.

That is huge! Jesus is your oasis, your constant source of refreshing, restoration, renewal, and replenishment. You don't ask Him for rest. You come to the One who *is* the rest you need. In life's wastelands, where no rain seems to fall, He is your spring of life-giving water. And when you face a long, untenable walk through the junkyard, He is your refuge from the dogs who try to intimidate and destroy you.

Jesus has not promised to make your life an oasis. He has promised to be your oasis. But you must come to Him and abide by staying with Him in the yoke. The idea grates against the American mind-set. In fact, the word *yoke* is practically anathema. We don't like bending our necks to be in lockstep with anyone. But He is not *anyone*! Notice how Jesus describes Himself: "I am gentle and lowly in heart, and you will find rest for your souls. For My yoke is easy and My burden is light" (Matt. 11:29 NKJV).

The Passion Translation talks about "joining with Jesus," which is what the yoke is really about. Jesus wants us to walk with Him in the purposeful way that two oxen walk together as they work in the fields. Jesus makes no apologies for the concept. Two things are absolutely certain: (1) He will never bend our necks to His yoke, and (2) He will never bend to our yoke.

How we handle Jesus' invitation is about our willingness to accept it as is. Will we allow our independence to be challenged or forfeit the benefits that come from abiding in Him? Whether consciously or not, we sometimes choose the latter. That could explain why so many of us are weary. We want Jesus to deliver, but we resist the process. We miss the simple truth that our oasis, Jesus, is in the yoke!

That is where I found Him after my first surgery went wrong. A week earlier, I agreed to get in the yoke with Him. Brain surgery was not my first choice, and the last thing I wanted was to leave Harvey and our beautiful family and church behind. Yet I decided that if surgery was God's choice, I would have surgery. And if God called me home, I would go home with joy. Whatever the outcome, my life was in the yoke, where He was.

Safety in the Yoke

Perhaps no part of my story describes the blessing of being yoked with Jesus more vividly than the one I'm about to share. After my fourth surgery, I was still in ICU and on a breathing tube, but I was conscious most of the time. However, my doctors and family knew something I did not yet know: that I had contracted a drug-resistant strain of pneumonia.

Do you remember the physical and spiritual realms I mentioned in my junkyard account? This story bridges them beautifully. While I was conscious, the Holy Spirit revealed potential danger ahead. What I saw was a window, and through it, a woman in a lab coat. She was visibly alarmed, which told me something was wrong. Because of where I was, it obviously involved my well-being.

As I watched, the woman blended various substances and ground them with her mortar and pestle. She was preparing a drug mixture, and I knew it was for me. Yet I had no idea why she was preparing it. Immediately, I wrote a note to Harvey: "They are messing with my medication and mixing meds for me. *This is not good!*"

The note puzzled Harvey. He already knew the doctors were working on a drug combination that would outsmart the pneumonia. He also knew that I was completely unaware of the issue, so he asked, "How did you know?"

"I saw it."

"Where did you see it?"

"Through the window," I answered.

The ICU unit was arranged with the nurses' station at the center and patients' rooms connected to it by windows. Through those windows, nurses could visually monitor their patients. Presumably, patients could also see into the nurses' station. My view was impaired, however, because I could not see into the nurses' station from my position in bed.

Harvey knew that and asked, "Deborah, how did you see it?"

He assumed that I was reporting what my physical eyes had seen. But what I described was happening in the spiritual realm. Once I made that clear, he became alarmed. I need to note here that Harvey is not known to be jumpy. But he is discerning. He recognized and validated my concern, asking, "Why is this a problem? What do you want me to do?"

I wrote, "Declare that no unholy thing can gain access to me or my body through that mixture, and declare that any drugs used will be for God's purposes only."

Harvey knew I was not asking him to embark on an esoteric exercise in spiritual warfare. I was responding in earnest to what the Holy Spirit revealed. The Lord was giving both of us the opportunity to agree with His will and cover in prayer an issue that we had not covered before. He did it so no demon or other wicked being could take opportunity when I was given the very powerful pharmaceutical cocktail that was being prepared.

When Harvey read my written request, he breathed a sigh of relief and said, "I can do that."

And he did! Not only did the medicine serve God's purposes, but this experience showed that what I saw in the spirit realm was not a drug-induced hallucination. I was in the yoke with the One who revealed what I needed to know. He did it to thwart any pharmaceutical threat ahead of time. And because I knew nothing about the pneumonia or the drug cocktail that was already being developed, Harvey knew that the Lord had allowed me to see what I described. Then our job was to agree that the mixture would serve God's purpose and conquer my pneumonia, in His power.

Knowledge, wisdom, and rescue are in the yoke!

YOKE FACTS

Getting in the yoke with Jesus is more than a spiritual concept. It is a multifaceted, real-time experience. That means it involves a learning process in which your circumstances eventually test what you have learned about God through His Word. As situations unfold, the truth that lives in your mind can become real in your life. That is the goal!

I am about to share several characteristics of getting in the yoke. At first glance, they might seem self-evident, but there is more to them than meets the eye. Consider each in terms of your own experiences. Doing this will help you to understand your responses to adversity, so take your time and jot down your thoughts as you go.

- Being in the yoke with Jesus means understanding the role you play in experiencing the rest He promises. You join yourself with Him by agreeing to function jointly with Him. This is about more than simple "do's" and "don'ts." It is more about imitating Christ, who is "gentle, humble, [and] easy to please" (Matt. 11:29 TPT).

- The yoke involves identifying so closely with Jesus that you function as He functions and move as He moves. Like Ginger Rogers following Fred Astaire's lead, your steps match Jesus' steps perfectly.

- In the yoke, you relate to Jesus not only as your Savior but also your Lord and Master. The issue of His Lordship is settled.

- Once in the yoke, you not only hear and obey, but you learn to share Jesus' outlook. Day by day and experience by experience, you see things more and more as He sees them, and you do things more as He would do them.

- When you are in Jesus' yoke, you understand that coming out from under it means leaving the oasis and returning to your wilderness of soul, the place where your peace is fragmented, and clarity is hard to come by. Conversely, when you let Him take the lead and carry the weight of the yoke, you find that life is pleasant and easy to bear.

What God Allows

As I write, *crisis* is a global byword. In mid-2019, it would have been difficult to imagine worldwide economic disruption and millions of deaths from a yet unheard-of virus. Such a crisis directly conflicts with our human desires and tests our belief systems. When the COVID-19 pandemic first took hold, we expected at some level to be relieved of its traumas quickly. The question is whether our expectations were realistic.

I'm not proposing a negative or fatalistic view of world events. Far from it. But once we recognized how transmissible the novel coronavirus was, we knew we had a tiger by the tail. Considering that we are a global society with many dense population centers (exactly what a contagion thrives on), we might have spared ourselves some strife and disillusionment by recognizing that the virus could stick around a while, even if we did everything humanly possible to contain it.

God knew the pandemic was coming. How sobering it is to think that He sometimes allows humankind to reap what it has sown. In other words, some adversity is the fruit of our long-term choices. Not all hardship starts that way, as we will see later on. But wherever our adversity originates, God will lead us—in it, through it, and out of it!

I can imagine Him saying, "Don't make this season more difficult than it needs to be. When I take you someplace you've never been or don't want to go, resist the urge to resist Me. Just stay in the yoke and come along with Me. *Trust Me.*"

That can be easier said than done. Because of cultural and historical norms in the United States (constitutionally guaranteed rights, rugged individualism, and personal independence), the American church finds total acceptance and trust difficult. Nevertheless, we can learn to yield to Jesus' yoke. Let's not emulate the Israelites by resenting our wilderness journey. Let's not exchange our freedom for the "leeks and onions" we enjoyed in our former enslavement. Let's not choose being in the yoke with Pharaoh over being joined with God. We are not exempt from being ensnared as the Israelites were. It happens when we forget our total dependence on God. That is when we bend away from His yoke and return to our wilderness places.

That is what happened when my peace and clarity evaporated. I had unwittingly pulled away from the yoke and usurped Jesus' role as Lord of my recovery. My only way forward was to face my independent streak and let the Lord walk me through a new landscape. I decided that He had allowed the changes I experienced, and I would learn from them what I could.

TAKEAWAYS FOR TAKING HIS YOKE

My prayer is that this chapter has dispelled some misunderstandings and helped you to see the beauty of being yoked with the Savior. I can promise you that there is no better way to walk through this life. Some of the points below have been mentioned already, but some are added for good measure. Take them to heart so they can work in and through your life.

- Coming to Jesus means coming into His presence. Being in His church and being a Christian are important, but unless you come to Jesus for yourself, you are missing the heart of His invitation (Matt. 11:28).

- Take stock of why you are coming to Jesus. Is it for what He has or for whom He is? Come for the latter, and you will gain the former.

- In dealing with your burdens, resist the reflex to bear down and try harder. This will only add to the weight you are already carrying.

- Remember that being born again and being yoked with Christ are not the same thing. To be yoked is to abide in Him, which implies not only receiving salvation but binding yourself to His will. Let His yoke determine your movements. That is the place of rest and rescue.

When you bend your neck to be in Jesus' yoke, He teaches you how to flourish. His instruction will never overburden or grind you down. Instead, it will protect you from the wear and tear of living by your own means. Trust Jesus in this! His motives are pure. He will never exploit, bully, misuse, or abuse you—*ever*. He will carry you through every difficulty and show you the whole truth about adversity.

LIVE AND LEARN

- Most likely, you have questions, questions, and more questions about some area of your life. How are your questions linked to your expectations? Which ones are driven by a sense that you "should have" done something differently? Are your "shoulds" reasonable, or are they keeping you in a state of unrest?

- Where have you moved from a sense of clarity to a state of confusion? Was the change caused by a "wild card" event that turned your world upside down, or by an internal, unrecognized change in your perspective? In either case, what truth will help to restore your bearings?

- What is the difference in your life between being born again and abiding in Christ? What is your personal cost of being in the yoke with Jesus? What are your personal (unique) benefits? How does staying in the yoke change your point of view, or how do you think it might?

3

THE PLAIN TRUTH
OF ADVERSITY

—◆—

*The righteous person faces many troubles, but the
LORD comes to the rescue each time.*

—*Psalms 34:19*

W hat we probably dislike most about adversity are the
curveballs it throws. When something like brain surgery goes haywire, the curveballs come fast. When my medical trajectory headed downward, my doctors were dismayed.
When my condition got stuck there, they became frustrated
and disheartened. By the fourth surgery, they were near panic
and realized what had been true all along—the situation was
out of their control.

I can only imagine how much they dreaded delivering one
troubling report after another. Usually, they gave Harvey the
news, and he conveyed it to me when my lucidity allowed. One
report was the "big one" we all hoped to avoid. After two unsuc-
cessful surgeries, I would have to undergo a third. But this time,
only a craniotomy would do. No one expected a second, and
now a third surgery, especially not one that involved removing
and reinserting a section of my skull. Nor had anyone dreamed
that a fourth surgery would soon come. Yet it did.

I thank God for preparing me to expect the unexpected and adjust to the curveballs that sailed my way. Harvey and I had done all that we knew to do. We had prayed and trusted the Lord's leading, both ahead of time and throughout the ordeal. Yet my path seemed to become more treacherous with every hour. We had to accept the options before us and make the best possible choices.

Handling the downturns was less daunting because the Lord had prepared us for them. That doesn't mean we never broke a sweat. Some of what happened was downright frightening, like when caregivers overfilled my feeding tube, and I began to vomit. That is not an easy feat when you are intubated! The usual exit route was obstructed, but the regurgitated material had to leave somehow. So it escaped through my eyes and nose. It was awful! Once the episode ended, the team stood me up and cleaned me off. I cannot describe how utterly helpless I felt. My caregivers weren't having much fun either.

For my loved ones, the chaos was vexing. Harvey and one of our daughters consistently invited the church and other supporters to pray. Whenever breakthroughs came, they shared the praise reports. Within hours, while everyone was still rejoicing, another setback would occur. Once again, the family would call everyone to prayer. The cycle was positively mystifying.

Once I was home and out of danger, one of our daughters and I talked about what happened. We got to the nub when she wondered aloud why my condition deteriorated even as people prayed more and more. She pointed out the elephant in the room, and it had to be addressed. We had seen the hand of God at every turn. We were absolutely certain that He had continually intervened. Yet many things went badly. How could that happen when God was so clearly involved?

As a pastor and a parent, I was distressed to think that my experiences might cause others to struggle in their faith. Would my partial loss of sight seem to nullify the healing testimony of Christ for some of them? Through years of ministry, I only wanted my life to glorify Him. Now I felt as though all of that had been undone. I cried out to the Lord, feeling like I had become a testimony to failure.

The thought was painful. The Lord understood and helped me to see the issue from a renewed perspective. "Yes," He said, "you stand as a testimony, not to failure but to strength, faith, and your love of Me. Those things glorify Me. The focus and purpose of your life have not been undone. I am not disappointed in you. You are My beloved, and I am well pleased."

The Lord did not reject me for the losses I experienced. Nor did He chide us for asking hard questions. He was not insulted because we wondered why things happened as they did. He simply helped us to understand the bigger picture, one beautiful moment at a time.

THE MYSTERY OF ADVERSITY

God is gentle with us and knows how we react to chaos: we put on our spiritual detective caps and search for the *who, what, when, where,* and *how* of it all. Until we find a way to explain what seems inexplicable, we classify our troubles as being unjust, meaningless, or even the fault of almighty God.

Some of our troubles are easy enough to explain because they result from choices we knew were risky. If I cruise down a narrow street at 150 mph, I am playing with fire, and I know it. If disaster strikes and I live to talk about it, I won't have to wonder what happened. But not every experience is so clear-cut. Even when we find answers, we don't necessarily find them all. Until we can accept that, we will feel unsettled.

Part of our quandary stems from our misunderstandings of adversity. Some of us were taught that if we behave "right," our lives will turn out "right." So we keep our scorecards up to date and claim to know what is ahead. Many of us have been taught that bad things only happen to bad people. (Of course, Jesus said in Mark 10:18 that no one but God is good, but that is a discussion for another time.) The fact is that adversity is marked by a degree of mystery, which simply means that we don't know everything God knows. If we can accept that and trust His faithfulness, the negative surprises we face will humble rather than intimidate us. Then we can bring our questions to the Father and search our own souls for any wrong assumptions we may have made.

Regardless of what we know and don't know, God knows the whole story. If He allows adversity to come, He does it from a larger and higher perspective than we can muster. He knows why He allowed it, and He knows that He made provision before we saw the trouble coming. He also knows what good will come from the trying of our faith. He sees what is at stake—not just our preferences and fears but also our need to grow and change.

A beautiful psalm gives us a sense of how all-encompassing God's knowledge is:

> *I can never escape from your Spirit! I can never get away from your presence! If I go up to heaven, you are there; if I go down to the grave, you are there. If I ride the wings of the morning, if I dwell by the farthest oceans, even there your hand will guide me, and your strength will support me. I could ask the darkness to hide me and the light around me to become night— but even in darkness I cannot hide from you. To you the night shines as bright as day. Darkness and light are the same to you (Psalms 139:7–12).*

Wherever you are and however dark your situation looks, God is there. You cannot fathom how deeply or how often He thinks about you! One of the most comforting verses in all of Scripture says, "You saw me before I was born. Every day of my life was recorded in your book. Every moment was laid out before a single day had passed" (Ps. 139:16).

What an astonishing statement that is, and how it transforms my outlook! When I feel completely broadsided, my heavenly Father maintains His perfect balance. Every day of my life is already in hand—*His hand.* He understands my alarm and pain, but He is neither shocked nor worried by events. I do not and cannot understand all the intricacies of my situation, but He does. He saw them coming, and He will see me through. If I know only that, I have all that I need.

KNOW WHAT YOU BELIEVE

Adversity is a test, and what you believe about adversity shows up when the test begins. If you see adversity as something to be avoided at all costs, your avoidance will show up in in your choices and their outcomes. But if you approach adversity as a challenge to be taken head-on, you will find in your hardship opportunities to become more resilient, more mature, and more compassionate. Either way, what you believe will become a self-fulfilling prophecy.

Knowing what you believe is critical where adversity is concerned. Most of us were raised on a mixed bag of beliefs, making our approach to difficulty unreliable. Then, when adversity rattles our cages, we arrive at mistaken conclusions. If you have ever felt that God abandoned you in your time of trouble, you know what I mean. It is easy to feel alone when you are surrounded by junkyard dogs. As they lick their chops, you might even believe that God is disciplining or correcting you. All your missteps come to mind: "I could have been a better wife. I'm not reading God's Word enough. I became fearful when I lost my job. My faith is so weak! No wonder I'm here. No wonder God has left me."

Another common misconception is that adversity comes to those who are weak in faith, as though tribulation can't touch us when faith is strong. That is a fallacy and a close cousin of the "right living" idea. It is based on two ideas: The first says that following Christ is a divine insurance policy against hardship. That cannot be true, because Jesus said, "Here on earth you will have many trials and sorrows. But take heart, because I have overcome the world" (John 16:33). The second idea is that we can perform our way into God's good graces. That can't be true either. Jesus rebuked the Pharisees' spiritual showboating. They thought their superficial law-keeping made them and God look good, as though He would ever take credit for the false impressions they tried to make!

Here is an idea that is true: every blessing is a gift from God, and His gifts come only by His grace. That is what the world needs to know. Every human being has struggles and needs, just like you and I do. They know that life can be hard. They have suffered setbacks. They distrust people who put on a good act. What can touch them is our transparency. Instead of being disappointed in us, they will be encouraged to know they're not the only ones going through "hell."

Your authentic witness is far more valuable than any contrived display of spirituality. The latter shines a light on you. That light can be unforgiving, and it does little good for anyone else. But your circumstances and your responses to hardship can help others by revealing the one true God. In your struggles, they can see that He lives and is intimately involved in the lives of real people.

That is what the wearied medical community witnessed in my case. They watched our family in the struggle. They saw our most difficult moments. They *knew* we were in a hard place, because they were too. They had played every card they had, to no avail. Instead of offering me hope and assurances, they finally realized they had nothing more to give. I remember a visit from my neurosurgeon when I was still in ICU. I was so glad to see him, but I was also concerned for him. I sensed the heavy burden on his shoulders and asked, "Are you doing OK, Doctor?"

He looked at Harvey and said, "Isn't this backwards? Shouldn't I be the one asking her if she is OK?"

We all had a good laugh, which was a blessing all by itself. But in that moment, God's love was revealed, ever so gently yet powerfully, to a man who desperately needed it.

FAITH IMPOSTERS

If knowing what you believe about adversity is crucial (which it is), so is knowing what you believe about faith. We sometimes exercise "faith" in ways that circumvent the very issues we need to face in faith. So let me tell you what faith is not. Faith is not a way to keep your sunny side up (although that will encourage you when the world seems to come apart at the seams). Faith is not an amulet to ward off evil. Nor is it a badge that entitles you to special privileges with God. Finally, faith is not an excuse to ignore reality or pretend that everything is OK when it isn't. That is called *denial*.

If anyone knows about faith, it is Jesus, our primary example of how to walk by faith. So what did He do when He faced unthinkable suffering and death? Did He declare that His faith would keep Him from going to the cross? Did He proclaim that angels would swoop down and carry Him out of danger? No! He faced the cross with eyes wide open, knowing that, even with its agonies, it was God's will. Without downplaying the difficulty, Jesus simply placed Himself in His Father's hands and did what the Father sent Him to do.

Faith is not a method of avoiding or denying unwanted circumstances. Instead, faith brings divine power to bear upon every situation and destructive work. Faith doesn't deny Satan's power. It *overcomes* it! Denying the presence of adversity does not glorify God. For one thing, it allows your troubles to fester and produce more suffering. It also fractures your testimony, because you can't deny your difficulty *and* credit God with delivering you from it.

There is one other faith fallacy to mention here. It is the idea of using faith to cover your fears. Have you ever lost a friend or loved one to cancer? Do you fear a similar fate? What would you do if you found a growth somewhere on your body? Would you see a doctor? Or would you ignore the issue and claim "by faith" that the growth has to disappear? I am not asking whether you believe in divine healing. I am assuming for the sake of argument that you do. What I am asking about is your motivation. Would you dismiss seeing a doctor because you fear bad news?

The question is so important! Faith that facilitates avoidance is not faith at all. It is fear. In the end, it will short circuit the real faith you need. When you stand in faith, you trust God to sustain you no matter what kind of trouble comes. You don't need to deny the possibility that something is wrong. You can put yourself in His hands, schedule an appointment with your doctor, and allow God to work in your life.

God is our refuge and strength, always ready to help in times of trouble. So we will not fear when earthquakes come and the mountains crumble into the sea. Let the oceans roar and foam. Let the mountains tremble as the waters surge! (Psalms 46:1–3)

Hidden Beliefs

We can always find opportunities to misunderstand our adversity. But when we pursue God, He gladly corrects our misunderstanding and reveals His truth. When I regained sufficient strength to ask the hard questions, I asked God about what my daughter and I had discussed: how things could have gone so wrong, despite His presence with us and despite all the prayer that had gone forth.

His answer seemed as clear as day: *spiritual warfare.* The Lord had prepared me for adversity for many reasons, some of which I did not recognize until later. He showed me that the enemy would contend for my life, and he did. But I was oblivious to the fact that I had given the enemy legal access to my health decades earlier. Back then, my youth and inexperience showed in something I said to God. It happened when Harvey's dad was diagnosed with an inoperable brain tumor. I loved my father-in-law so much that I could not bear the thought of his dying. So I prayed fervently and told God that if He would heal my father-in-law, I would be willing to bear his tumor for him.

My zeal was completely off base. Only one Person was qualified to bear the sicknesses of others. That is Jesus Christ. In my ignorance, I agreed to accept a brain tumor. I thought I was bargaining with God, which is never a good idea. Actually, I'd made a deal with the devil, and he was happy to accept my terms!

God is more gracious than I could ever deserve. Although I gave the enemy carte blanche to plant and even guard a tumor in my brain, the Lord protected my life. Once I realized what I'd done all those years ago, I broke agreement with my foolishness and repented of it. When I did, I barred the enemy's legal access to my brain.

To be clear, not every difficulty you endure can be traced to a long-forgotten pact you have made with the prince of darkness. If you insist on believing it can, you will spend your life condemning yourself for things you may or may not have done! Scripture says that God "gives his sunlight to both the evil and the good, and he sends rain on the just and the unjust alike" (Matt. 5:45). Adversity is a fact of life. To maintain a balanced view, just accept that and acknowledge any careless thoughts, words, or actions that might be inviting unnecessary heartache. Then, you can leave it with the Lord and entrust yourself to His faithfulness.

He Will Deliver You

We started this chapter with an important scripture. Now let's read it in the English Standard Version: "Many are the afflictions of the righteous, but the LORD delivers him out of them all" (Ps. 34:19). There is such wisdom in that verse! On the one hand, there is no doubt that the righteous will suffer afflictions (many afflictions). Yet the Lord will deliver the righteous from *all* of them!

Notice that He delivers you from hardship; He did not say that He prevents you from experiencing hardship. It is so important to remember this, especially when adversity breathes down your neck and false expectations breed doubt, dismay, and resignation. For example, if you believe that God should deliver you before trouble comes, you will approach your difficulty in self-defeating ways. Instead of putting yourself in His hands (which is an act of trust), you might believe that He has wronged you (a sign of distrust).

Of course, the devil will accuse God of breaking His promise to deliver you, when God did nothing of the sort. When you believe those accusations, you heap frustration on yourself. You cannot help but fluctuate between confidence in God's promises and "evidence" of His faithlessness, making it harder to lean in when you need Him most. When trouble comes, you cannot afford to harbor any sense of confusion, anger, or abandonment. Being in a storm is hard. Being at odds with God is much harder.

Purpose in the Storm

Do you remember when Jesus and His disciples got caught in a storm? Jesus had just healed a leper, a centurion's slave, Peter's mother-in-law, and many others. Then He and His disciples set out on the water, and a storm broke out. When the disciples cowered in fear, Jesus chided them, saying, "Why are you such cowards, such faint-hearts?" (Matt. 8:26 MSG). Then He stood up and spoke to the elements. "'Silence!' [He said, and] the sea became smooth as glass" (Matt. 8:26 MSG).

The storm came to oppose Jesus and His team. God didn't cause the storm; the storm was designed to thwart God's plan. When you are walking in Jesus' will for the kingdom and for your life, opposition will come, not from God but from the enemy of your soul. Notice also that the storm in Matthew 8 came at a significant time. Jesus had been healing and delivering suffering people, and He was heading to the Gadarenes where demoniacs ruled and wreaked chaos. The storm was designed to paralyze the disciples in fear and prevent Jesus from crossing the lake. The enemy did not want Him to deliver the demoniacs. Nor did he want the chaos in the region to end. Deliverance would only upset the rule of darkness, and Satan never wants that!

Your storms also come at significant times. The enemy wants the timing to work against you and against God. But it works against the enemy! When Jesus silences the storm that tries to cut you down in significant moments, He reveals God's glory more powerfully. The more intense the adversity, the more His power is revealed, in and through you. The more grueling the trial, the more glory God gets and the more powerfully you become knitted to Him. You realize that He has not abandoned you but has shown up in astonishing ways. You learn that He has not sent trouble as a response to your failure, but the enemy sent trouble because you are fulfilling God's will. Knowing this frees you from the need to perform and helps you to live in "the unforced rhythms of grace" (Matt. 11:29 MSG). From that glorious position, you will see adversity more and more as God sees it.

LIVE AND LEARN

- Which recent events in your life would you classify as "curve balls"? Did they cause you to break a sweat (feel troubled, frightened, or confused)? Which event seemed most confusing, and why?

- What do you find most worrisome about adversity? Is it that you don't know how much longer your adversity will last? Are you afraid that you won't be able to handle the situation if it worsens? From the "Know What You Believe" section, choose the misunderstanding that has most affected your experiences with adversity, and consider its impact in a particular situation.

- Where might denial be showing up in your life? How might it be connected to fear? Consider the timing of a current or recent trial; what might it suggest?

PART II

Walking It Out

4

SEEING AS GOD SEES

———◆———

Open my eyes so I can see what you show me of your
miracle-wonders.

—Psalms 119:18 MSG

U nexpected changes have a way of getting and even holding
our attention, especially when we lose what is precious.
As 2018 drew to a close, my obvious goals were to rise above my
adversity, adjust my thinking where needed, and continue my
recovery. So before the new year dawned, I took time to reflect
on all that had happened and all that it meant. Without hesitation, I concluded that 2018 had been a year of adversity, and I
was glad to wave it goodbye.

The Holy Spirit nudged me and asked, "What about the
miracles?"

In His mercy, God let me know that my conclusion was
incomplete. Immediately, I felt deep conviction and gratitude.
He was right, of course. As hard as the year had been, it was
filled with miracles. For one, my heavenly Father snatched me
from the jaws of death! He also provided for every imaginable need, and He protected me from even more serious losses.
There had been much adversity; but there was much more to
remember than that.

The Holy Spirit's question exposed a gap between how I saw my trial and how He saw it. I saw the difficulties, but He focused on the miracles. I saw the losses, and He saw redemption. With a single question, He lifted me from a disheartened, dead-end perspective into a hopeful, life-giving one. The lesson could not be clearer: He and I had seen the same situation in two entirely different ways.

Check Your Eyes

In his paraphrase of Matthew 6:22–23, the late Eugene Peterson found exquisite words to describe the ways in which we can choose to see:

> *Your eyes are windows into your body. If you open your eyes wide in wonder and belief, your body fills up with light. If you live squinty-eyed in greed and distrust, your body is a dank cellar. If you pull the blinds on your windows, what a dark life you will have! (MSG)*

The passage is so visual and so deftly explained some of what I had experienced! By the end of 2018, my wide eyes of wonder and belief were becoming squinty—so much so that I wanted to stash the whole exhausting brain-surgery episode in a cold-storage compartment of forgetfulness.

Do you see how my perspective shaped my outlook? Even though I had continually acknowledged God's goodness throughout the ordeal, my losses dominated my look back. My memory was selective; therefore, my conclusions were skewed. Had God not challenged my viewpoint, the loss of physical sight might have produced in me a chronic state of discouragement and even bitterness.

This is a classic example of what happens when you don't see events the way God sees them. I'm not suggesting that we ought to arrive at a place of pristine or divine vision. We are human, after all. But I am talking about a process of seeing our experiences more objectively and completely. That is important, because how we interpret them will ultimately determine our quality of life.

It is easy to default to the negative. We are naturally drawn to seeing what's wrong, and we can easily become fixated on it. This is especially true when we agonize over our troubles. We become anxious over depleted health, energy, or finances. We grieve over the loss of loved ones. And we yearn for normalcy to replace our chaos. Acknowledging these feelings is important. But we also need to test our perspectives and seek God's help in adjusting them. Instead of pining for what used to be, we can purposefully occupy our minds with Him and with where He is leading us. When we do that, the future doesn't seem fearful or intimidating. The presence of our enemies does not loom large when our focus is on our God.

I am not advocating a mind-over-matter exercise that ignores what you are up against. We talked about the big fat lie called *denial*, and I'm 100 percent against it. I am simply speaking to something over which we have considerable control, and that is our way of seeing and interpreting what we see. Sometimes, in cases of extreme or continuous trauma, we need help in adjusting our perspectives. Professional counsel can be part of God's provision in such cases. For example, if you have experienced the trauma of war or have lived in an abusive situation for an extended period of time, go ahead and ask for the help you need to recover. Don't be ashamed to enlist the services of those whom God gifts and equips to assist you. I have worked with many, many people who have been deeply scarred by abuse. I do not minimize their suffering or their needs. Our heavenly Father has made provision for them and for all who are hurting.

Focus on the Shepherd

Every January, people around the world make resolutions, buy exercise equipment, clean out closets, start new diets, commit to new Bible-reading plans, and promise to change. As often as not, the exercise equipment gathers dust, the closet comes undone, and the resolutions unravel before February is over. The reason is simple: even when our intentions are forward-looking, our focus can be locked in the past. We desire the new, but the old point of view grips us. Instead of experiencing change, we rehash what happened and drag our painful memories into our tomorrows.

The only way to change our lives is to change our way of seeing. And the only way to do that is to keep our eyes on Jesus. Peter learned this in dramatic fashion. He witnessed Jesus' manner. He saw Jesus' compassion and miracles. He experienced His authenticity and consistent character. Peter learned day by day that when Jesus said something, the disciples could count on it. So when he watched Jesus walk on water in the middle of a storm, Peter called out, "Lord, if it's really you, tell me to come to you, walking on the water" (Matt. 14:28).

What Peter said was revolutionary! He saw Jesus doing what no man or woman had ever done, and he wanted to do it too. When Jesus said, "Come," Peter stepped onto the choppy seas and walked! In that moment, he did not focus on the storm but on the Good Shepherd. He set aside the distractions that ordinarily dictated his decisions, and he did the impossible.

If you know the story, you know that Peter's newfound focus did not last very long. He soon "saw the strong wind and the waves, he was terrified and began to sink" (Matt. 14:30). When he took his eyes off Jesus and put them back on the storm, the walking ended, and the sinking began. (I say that with all deference to Peter; he deserves credit for provoking Jesus' invitation and then walking on water, even for a moment!)

Seeing the possibility was the table Jesus prepared for that moment in Peter's life. And Peter feasted on it! He only saw what Jesus had prepared because he was focused on Jesus. King David never walked on water, but he understood this idea and wrote, "You prepare a table before me in the presence of my enemies" (Ps. 23:5 NKJV). David knew that the opposition was always present, but he feasted anyway. His eyes were on the One who prepared the feast, not whatever or whoever wanted to keep him from receiving it.

When you focus on the Shepherd, the table is visible, and your trust keeps you feeding on that which He prepared for you. He feeds your soul when you need it most, strengthening your resistance to moments of weakness and enabling you to think outside the box. That is Peter's story. While he kept his eyes on Jesus, the storm lost its power to limit him. But when his focus slipped, he placed Jesus at the periphery and brought the opposition front and center in his field of vision.

It's simple: you see like Jesus when you focus on Him. He expands your vision and opens your horizons. You cannot look at Him and stay squinty-eyed. It is when your focus moves away from Jesus that your way of seeing hardens, and your thinking hardens with it. When you fix your eyes on the enemies all around you, your perspective automatically narrows until all you can see is adversity and loss.

That is where I was when the Holy Spirit nudged me. I experienced the kind of shaking we all face at some point. If you are there now, give yourself credit for whatever water-walking you have done. (In times of deep sorrow, that could include taking your next breath.) And if you feel yourself sinking, just turn your eyes back to Jesus. Remember how trustworthy He is. Let your dependence on Him flourish and shrink your fear of the storm. Adjust your focus until you see your position in relation to Him, not in relation to your adversaries.

Bear in mind that when your vision wanders unchecked, your spiritual condition becomes more of a problem than your troubles ever were. Instead of feeding from God's table, your spiritual state *feeds you to your enemies.* That is not what you were created for. You were created to overcome them. So keep your eyes on Jesus!

THE IDOLATRY TRAP

When life bears down on you, idolatry is the last thing you want to hear about. Do you remember when the Israelites made a golden calf in the wilderness? (See Exodus 32.) It was a classic example of idolatry. But not all idolatry looks like that. Idolatry is more common today than we realize, with or without a golden calf. Statues and rituals are only symptoms of idolatry. The actual sin of idolatry is about making anything but God your primary focus.

Whatever preoccupies your thinking can become an idol: your career, spouse, fitness regimen, wardrobe, the food you eat, or even your children. I have been convicted in the area of my children more than once. Like most parents, I love my kids fiercely. When they face difficult choices, I can easily get entangled in worry. When I do, my focus quietly shifts away from Jesus and toward whatever I think the trouble is. The change is subtle at first. I love the Lord, and I put my children in His hands with all the intentionality I can muster. Yet I sometimes get overly absorbed by my concern for them. When I do, I know that my trust is not placed squarely in Him. I'm not seeing their issues the way He sees them.

That is how deception works, and idolatry is based in deception. It sneaks up on you and consumes your thought life, your prayer life, and your whole soul (your mind, will, and emotions)! That is a sure sign that you are not seeing the situation God's way. Somehow, you have made something other than

God your primary focus, and whatever that "something" is, it is an idol.

So what does idolatry cost you? It gives the enemy legal access to your life, particularly in the area that is consuming your attention. When you are in this condition, you are your biggest problem and your worst enemy. Because your focus is away from God and on your troubles, you cannot see His table of provision clearly, and you cannot enjoy the feast! Instead of allowing Him to lift your worries from your shoulders, you force the burden on yourself. You might not notice the shift in your perspective, but you find yourself thinking, "If I don't get a handle on this, something terrible is going to happen."

When that is your view of your circumstances, the enemy has you right where he wants you. He knows it is a matter of time before you entertain self-sabotaging thoughts: "Is God unwilling to hear my prayers? Are they falling on deaf ears? Has He removed His provision from me?" Sooner or later, you will ask, "Why are You letting this happen, Lord?"

God understands that such questions reveal our pain, but they are not grounded in the truth of who He is or who we are in Christ. It is not that we intentionally worship someone or something other than Yahweh. We simply divert our primary attention from Him and find ourselves worshipping idols by default. I said earlier that this is an area over which we have significant control. We control our vision; therefore, we have the power to put our eyes back on Jesus. Then we can see as He sees, and His table of provision becomes clear.

OWN YOUR DISTRACTION

To break the cycle of misplaced vision and see your adversity the way God sees it, just acknowledge your drift into idolatry. Then repent and be reconciled with the mandate to "love God, your God, with your whole heart: love him with all that's in you, love him with all you've got!" (Deut. 6:5 MSG). Admit that you cannot do this while you are consumed with your problems. By owning your distraction, you can break agreement with its power to draw you away from God and His table.

That is the perfect opportunity to worship Him—not by going through the motions, but by sincerely cultivating His presence. As you do, you'll experience His love, power, and direction pouring forth. He will infuse you with His strength and empower you to withstand whatever difficult circumstances you face. With your focus restored, your way of thinking can shift toward victory and away from defeat.

This is what the Lord offered me as 2019 approached. He knew that if I memorialized the previous year as one of adversity rather than miracles, I would progressively seed my heart with hopelessness and despair. So He fine-tuned my vision and showed me the way forward.

Understanding as God Understands

One of the challenges we face in seasons of adversity is a lack of understanding, which only feeds our pain. The more we cultivate God's perspective, the less space we give to confusion, angst, self-pity, and other self-defeating conditions. Then we can become increasingly God-reliant and less prone to evaluating our circumstances through earthly knowledge. Instead, we open ourselves to the pure wisdom of God.

This is what Job learned during his terrible season of adversity. He was a godly man whom God described as "the finest man in all the earth" and "blameless—a man of complete integrity" (Job 1:8). The Lord said that Job "fears God and stays away from evil" (Job 1:8).

Satan replied the only way the accuser can:

Yes, but Job has good reason to fear God. You have always put a wall of protection around him and his home and his property. You have made him prosper in everything he does. Look how rich he is! But reach out and take away everything he has, and he will surely curse you to your face! (Job 1:9–11)

Satan accused Job of being faithless and using God. God knew better and granted Satan permission to test Job's faith. Eager to prove God wrong, Satan wreaked havoc in Job's life. Raiders stole Job's livestock and killed his farmhands. Fire burned up his sheep and all of his shepherds. More raiders stole his camels and killed more of his servants. A wind knocked down the house where his children had gathered, killing all ten of them. Then boils covered Job's body and he agonized in pain. When it seemed things could get no worse, Job's wife sniped, "Are you still trying to maintain your integrity? Curse God and die" (Job 2:9).

The poor man was utterly grief-stricken and baffled by what befell him. To add insult to injury, the friends who came to comfort him decided that his suffering was God's judgment for his sin. Job wasn't the least bit comforted to hear that! And His friends got it wrong anyway. They did not see his situation the way God saw it. None of them considered Satan's role in Job's troubles, not even Job. This added to the confusion and gave God a bad name.

In their defense, Job and his friends did not have all the teaching and resources we have today. Yet even modern believers make the same mistake they did. Barna Research found that "four out of ten Christians (40%) strongly agreed that Satan 'is not a living being but is a symbol of evil.'"[1] Other people believe that he exists; but they also believe that he will leave them alone if they don't bother him. Still others believe that talking about Satan glorifies him. Perhaps they also believe that ignoring him glorifies God.

These unscriptural ideas can only distort your view of adversity and cause others to misunderstand your struggle. I remember some believers wondering how a simple medical procedure by a top-notch neurosurgeon left me blinded in one eye. The situation seemed "out of this world," so they concluded that it was God's doing. I know they sincerely believed what they were saying, but they sincerely misunderstood God!

Sometimes, when chaos is hard to explain, we assume that the afflicted person's faith is below standard in some way. This not only adds to the confusion, but it increases the person's suffering. I have learned that trying to put this misunderstanding to rest is often futile, so I leave the matter with God. I have to trust that when others doubt or blame me, He knows the truth. Carrying the grief of their accusations is not something I can afford to do.

This takes us back to the question of why God allows our trials and, more specifically, why He allowed Job's suffering. I believe God trusted Job, saw the long game, and allowed Job's story to teach us about adversity. God knew that His love and righteousness would prevail over all evil. In fact, He blessed Job even more than before his trouble started.

DOUBLE-MINDEDNESS

God never vacillates or feels at odds with Himself. He is never confused, conflicted, or indecisive. We can be all those things at times, but the more we see through His eyes, the more His truth becomes wisdom to us, conforming us to His ways even further. James said it this way:

> *If you don't know what you're doing, pray to the*
> *Father. He loves to help. You'll get his help, and won't*

be condescended to when you ask for it. Ask boldly, believingly, without a second thought. People who "worry their prayers" are like wind-whipped waves. Don't think you're going to get anything from the Master that way, adrift at sea, keeping all your options open. (James 1:5–8 MSG).

Single-mindedness produces stability. A single-minded person is not "blown and tossed by the wind" (James 1:6), but indecision blows the double-minded person every which way. Simple actions become complicated and receiving from God becomes difficult. This instability is not a sign that God has deserted you. It simply reveals your inner conflict.

I believe that double-mindedness comes from two particular choices: one is straddling the fence between trust in God and trust in the world system, and the other is clinging to your reasoning and judgment as you try to trust God. I am not suggesting that you check your mind at the door. God gave you a brain so you would use it. However, your intellect can only take you so far. You know what you know, and you have no idea what you don't know.

We need God! If you are plagued by double-mindedness, there is a cure: ask the Lord to give you the wisdom He promised and open His Word to you. Then follow through. It's one thing to hear what God has to say, but until you act on it, your situation will not change. You will be tempted to bounce back and forth between conflicting opinions, worsening your double-mindedness and adding to your frustration.

If double-mindedness is painful (which it certainly is), why don't we end it? For one thing, we are often terrified of making mistakes. For another, we dislike making commitments. So we work hard to keep our reputations shiny and our options open. Our fear of making mistakes doesn't always happen consciously, but the refusal to commit does. Either way, double-mindedness is a trap. Recognize it when it shows up and seek the scriptural truth that reflects God's holistic viewpoint. Don't let a divided heart wear you out and keep you stuck in situations you tired of long ago.

We know that God causes everything to work together for the good of those who love God and are called according to his purpose for them (Romans 8:28).

Keep These Thoughts in Mind

From this chapter, you can draw conclusions that will help you to see your adversity more and more as God sees it. The following is a list of general thoughts, but you can add whatever specific ideas came to mind while you were reading.

- Job's life proves that adversity does not always result from sin. His life also settles any questions about the devil's existence and his work to steal, kill, and destroy (John 10:10).

- When you see adversity as God sees it, you can rest assured that it has nothing to do with whether God loves you or is powerful enough to help you. It *is* about a bigger purpose for what you're going through, and that bigger purpose will result in evil being turned for good (Rom. 8:28).

- God's goodness is far greater than the devil's plan to harm or humiliate you. Don't stress out over being unjustly treated or misunderstood. God always has the last word. Rest in Him and He will position you for restoration and greater blessing. Allow your trust in Him to dispel your confusion, grief, anguish, and impatience; and let it make room for the peace that passes understanding (Phil. 4:7).

I pray that this chapter has opened your vision and increased your understanding of the struggles you face. If you are disheartened in this moment, keep reading! You will be en*courage*d!

LIVE AND LEARN

- Do you feel (or have you ever felt) pressured to get a handle on your situation or risk being ruined by it? What is that situation, and how do you think it could ruin you? Might you be trusting the problem more than you trust the Good Shepherd? How would things change if you flipped that equation?

- Where is your focus right now? Is it on the Good Shepherd and the table He has prepared for you? Or is it on the enemies and/or challenges you are facing? (Remember that people are not your enemies, according to Ephesians 6:12.) Ask the Lord to reveal Himself and His provision. How might what He shows you change any present difficulty?

- Where are the "idolatry traps" in your life? Which one has cost you the most, and why? How might double-mindedness have contributed to your idolatry? What concrete steps can you take to own this sin, repent, and move on?

5

TAKE COURAGE

—◆—

Be on guard. Stand firm in the faith. Be courageous. Be strong. And do everything in love.
            —*1 Corinthians 16:13–14*

Courage. We see it in the news, in history books, and in everyday life. It is "the quality of being ready and willing to face negative situations involving danger or pain."[2] People of courage choose bravery in spite of the consequences. With physical courage, they endure bodily hardship, pain, death, and the threat of death. With moral courage, they choose what is right and honorable, even when it brings opposition, shame, scandal, or personal loss.

Whatever form it takes, courage is essential in adversity. That is why the Lord told Joshua to "be strong and courageous" (Josh. 1:6). His mentor and leader, Moses, had just died, and Joshua was about to step into his shoes. Victory was ahead, but so was warfare. The Lord prepared His servant's heart for the challenge. He knew that among the enemies Joshua would face in the Promised Land, there was one that his mentor encountered all the way through the wilderness. That enemy is *discouragement*, and courage is its antidote.[3]

Humans first lost their courage after Adam and Eve ate the fruit of deception. Ever since, even the bravest of heroes has known discouragement. Faithful men and women of God have been overwhelmed by it: Rachel and Hannah were devastated by their barrenness. King David was crushed by his son Absalom's death. Elijah was so discouraged by Jezebel's threats that he wanted to die, even after witnessing God's great victory on Mount Carmel!

No one is exempt from discouragement—not your best friend, boss, or even your pastor. When my medical team overfilled my feeding tube, a feeling of helplessness flooded my soul. In other words, I felt discouraged! When I arrived home from the hospital, my depth perception was off. Walking was tricky. Half of my peripheral vision was gone, and yes—discouragement came calling. I hadn't forgotten the miracles God had done, but I did grieve for what I'd lost. The grieving was perfectly normal and necessary. The important thing was to avoid becoming mired in it.

Discouragement is real and very challenging; but it is not a life sentence. For me, taking courage was a process of making adjustments, not only where my physical eyes were concerned, but in my spiritual sight. I needed to remember how God saw my struggle and how His *en*couragement was available in every circumstance.

Even Moses?

The Bible does not downplay discouragement. The man God chose to lead the Israelites out of Egypt got discouraged, even though God was with him throughout his life. Moses reached his wits' end more than once. At one point, he told God, "I cannot carry all these people by myself. The burden is too heavy for me. If this is how you are going to treat me [God], please go ahead and kill me—if I have found favor in your eyes—and do not let me face my own ruin" (Num. 11:14–15 NIV).

Isn't that amazing? The man with whom God partnered in an astounding historical and spiritual event actually asked God to kill him! In today's vernacular, Moses had a meltdown. Was it because God forgot or rejected him? No! It was God's favor that caused his meltdown. The Lord Himself trusted Moses to lead millions of people to freedom, which Moses must have appreciated. Yet the assignment overwhelmed him. He became downcast because his destiny was so great.

That might seem absurd, but only if you forget that Bible characters are human beings. Moses believed he was in a lose/lose situation. On the one hand, God expected so much of him. And on the other, the people demanded that he keep them happy. Imagine trying to satisfy all the demands of six million people—for forty years! Even when God used Moses to free them from slavery, they griped about the leeks they left behind. They refused to be content. But their discontentment had little to do with Moses. They treated God the same way. They built a golden calf and worshipped it instead of Him!

Not surprisingly, Moses saw himself as a failure more than once. So he begged God, "If I have found favor in your eyes … do not let me face my own ruin" (Num. 11:15 NIV). In other words, "If You are going to hold me responsible for the attitudes and behaviors of all these people, please put me out of my misery now."

If Moses could be discouraged, so can we. But we can learn from his example. Imperfect as he was, Moses did the right thing with his meltdown: he brought it to God and admitted resenting the great responsibility God had given him. He then made God a flawed but honest offer: "If You care about me at all, kill me before this assignment ruins me."

Moses did what we often do: he fell victim to one of discouragement's most insidious symptoms: the tendency to question whether God even cares about our struggles. Remember all that God and Moses had shared together, including their meeting at the burning bush and the ten plagues that countered Pharaoh's resistance—not to mention the fact that God had saved the baby Moses from the massacre of Hebrew children! Moses had the most amazing experiences with God, yet he was not convinced that God cared about him.

Moses' problem had less to do with his situation than with how he saw it. As long as he focused on adversity and impossibility, discouragement would overshadow his belief that God had his back, even though God proved His faithfulness again and again. That is exactly why Moses began losing hope in delivering the people into the Promised Land. The clouding of his perspective chased away his courage, making it hard for him to "face negative situations involving danger or pain."[4]

Are you in a similar spot? Are you discouraged and dwelling on the negative aspects of your life or calling? Maybe you wonder whether God cares. Maybe you are exhausted and losing sight of His power and grace. You are no less human than Moses was. You too can be tempted to blame God for entrusting you with His divine plans. If you become distraught, it is probably less about the level of difficulty and more about your perspective—how you see where you are, who you are, and who God is in your life. He understands your resentment, but He knows it can only drive you when your vision is limited to what your physical eyes can see.

If that is where you are, don't worry! This is a great time to adjust your outlook. God did say He would never leave or forsake you, right? And you know that you can go to Him when you are weary. (See Hebrews 13:5 and Matthew 11:28.) He is powerful and full of grace, even if you don't "feel it." So remind yourself of these things! Take your meltdown to Jesus or you will be tempted to bail out—not only from your current situation but potentially from every situation that seems less than perfect.

Courage, Faith, and Expectations

The cure for discouragement is not the absence of fear. It is the presence of courage. There is no courage where fear is not present. When the Allied Forces landed at Normandy in 1944, they knew the enemy was waiting to cut them down. Every warrior who stepped onto the beach did so through a hail of bullets. They had traveled overnight through rough seas, and many were sick from the journey. Now they were human targets with nowhere to hide. Yet they headed toward the gunfire. They fought despite their fear.

These heroes displayed physical and moral courage, but some approached their mission with spiritual courage as well. That is, they coupled their courage with faith. This is something the American church doesn't talk about very often. So many churches teach that the "stronger" your faith is, the fewer your challenges will be. The idea is alluring but unscriptural, and it leads to false expectations. I believe it is the reason so many people think that Christianity "isn't working" for them. Instead of expecting God to be their strength, they expect Him to swoop down like a superhero and remove them from all difficulty. They don't realize that they need to respond with courage. Instead of wanting God to bail them out of trouble, they need to do what He asked, wait for His answers to their believing prayers, and be satisfied when He answers according to His will, character, and nature—not their own.

When I served full-time as a biblical counselor, I worked with many people, some of whom had suffered horrific abuse. As varied as their histories were, discouragement was perhaps the issue that all of them faced. In some cases of profound trauma, discouragement was virtually unavoidable. Often, however, it was based on what a client thought should happen. Because their expectations were unbiblical, they were bound to be disappointed, regardless of their circumstances.

Now, after many years as a pastor, I have seen people who are discouraged and uncertain about what's next. That is understandable. What is interesting is how it contrasts with what Harvey and I have seen in the developing world. Most of the people there are far less discouraged, even in the persecuted church. We often work in areas where poverty runs rampant and living conditions are deplorable. Yet the people are encouraged more often than not.

Why would poor, oppressed, and even persecuted people be less prone to discouragement than we Americans are? I believe it is because their expectations are more grounded than ours. They are well aware of the adversity they face on every side. They don't expect to be exempted from difficulty or guaranteed smooth sailing. They fully understand the need to mix their faith with courage, and they know that no one can do it for them. As far as they are concerned, their well-being, the future, and even their survival depend on it.

Because people in oppressed regions see their situations clearly, they are highly motivated to stand and take courage. They do it as an act of their will, but they don't do it alone. They partner with God, they trust in His strength, and they keep going! That is faith, and it pleases God (Heb. 11:6). He then releases His miracle empowerment, which gives them joy and fuels their commitment to Him and His will!

Nehemiah continued, "Go and celebrate with a feast of rich foods and sweet drinks, and share gifts of food with people who have nothing prepared. This is a sacred day before our Lord. Don't be dejected and sad, for the joy of the LORD is your strength" (Nehemiah 8:10).

Joshua Took Courage

The Lord prepares us for what is ahead. While Moses was alive, He prepared Joshua for his future role as Moses' replacement. Then, as we have seen, God spoke to Joshua about how to proceed into the Promised Land, not as Moses' second in command, but as his successor:

> No man shall be able to stand before you all the days of your life; as I was with Moses, so I will be with you. I will not leave you nor forsake you. Be strong and of good courage, for to this people you shall divide as an inheritance the land which I swore to their fathers to give them. Only be strong and very courageous, that you may observe to do according to all the law which Moses My servant commanded you; do not turn from it to the right hand or to the left, that you may prosper wherever you go. This Book of the Law shall not depart from your mouth, but you shall meditate in it day and night, that you may observe to do according to all that is written in it. For then you will make your way prosperous, and then you will have good success. Have I not commanded you? Be strong and of good courage; do not be afraid, nor be dismayed, for the LORD your God is with you wherever you go (Joshua 1:5–9 NKJV).

Three times in one brief exchange, God told Joshua to be courageous. When God tells you to act in a particular way, you can trust that He has already made provision for you to obey. His words to Joshua indicate that courage was available. God was not giving advice or asking Joshua to do the impossible. He was offering to give Joshua the very thing He commanded him to choose: courage. The question was not whether God would provide what Joshua needed but whether Joshua would take what God had provided.

Notice that God did not promise to eliminate the difficulties ahead. In fact, His promise showed Joshua that taking the Promised Land would be difficult. Why else would he need to be brave? But God assured Joshua that he would succeed. Over time, the promise would also help Joshua to resist discouragement. God knew that Joshua would face anxiety-producing circumstances, and He did not expect Joshua to face them alone. God would partner with him, as He had with Moses. And God would provide him with the supernatural strength he needed to accomplish what God commissioned him to do. Joshua's part was to combine his faith with courage and do God's bidding.

Remember that the divine mandate was to take the Promised Land from the people who already lived there. Joshua knew what that meant: conflict, danger, and plenty of uncertainty. Neither he nor Moses had an easy time as leaders, but both men accomplished outstanding things for God and His people. Their stories remind us that, as children who trust God, we can do amazing things, no matter what.

How Fear Lies to You

Taking courage means following and obeying God when fear tempts us to quit. Fear is a thief and liar that has lied to good people and stolen destinies. At the height of his troubles, Job said, "What I always feared has happened to me. What I dreaded has come true" (Job 3:25). The Scriptures don't describe every fear that Job entertained before tragedy struck. However, Job admitted that what befell him made him afraid *before* any of it happened.

That is the dark power of fear! It invites the enemy to access your life. Remember that Satan is not omnipotent. He cannot arbitrarily heap destruction on you. But he can access your life to the extent that you cooperate with him. And you cooperate with him by elevating your fears over your trust in the Lord. Fear is a form of agreement with the enemy. It always expects the worst, which is exactly what he has in mind. So he diligently calls your attention to whatever can breed fear in your heart.

Imagine for the sake of example that everyone on your father's side of the family has died of a heart attack. (Remember, this is a fictitious example, not a prophecy!) Now, imagine that you are fit and healthy, but the devil reminds you daily of how your relatives perished. What is he doing? He is pressing you to open an access point through fear. Then, once he has your attention, he inspires a family member to remind you of the family history and ask whether you've had a stress test lately. Soon another relative sends an article that gives you a detailed list of every heart attack symptom!

Are you getting the picture? The devil is a relentless schemer (Eph. 6:11). Once he plants fear in your heart, he picks a particularly vulnerable moment in which to draw your attention to the symptoms he already advertised. He cannot give you a heart attack. But he is an experienced counterfeiter who specializes in bogus symptoms. When you feel the slightest twinge, all of his earlier suggestions come cascading to your mind. Then, because you fear imminent disaster, your mind works to accommodate your expectations. And what do you expect? The worst, because that is what the enemy suggested all along. Through nothing more than manipulation, he can position you to open the door to disease and even death.

How do you take courage in such a situation? You do it by being intentional, decisive, and swift to refute anything that challenges the truth of God. The next time your fearful family members "prophesy" doom, tell them that you are trusting God's protection against anything He has not authored. After reading the symptom list sent by your well-meaning relative, declare that you were healed by the stripes of Jesus (Isa. 53:5) and are not open to symptoms of a heart attack or any other ailment, in Jesus' name. Then, when counterfeit symptoms strike, you can immediately claim the protection of Jesus' blood and refuse to agree with fear or infirmity.

Whenever the enemy tries to flood your mind with premonitions of tragedy, praise God aloud. Pray, read His Word, and say whatever He says about your well-being. Realize that you are most vulnerable to Satan's pranks in times of adversity. When your trajectory takes a wrong turn, it becomes easier to believe that a downward spiral has begun. You can also be tempted to see your adversity as a sign that God is angry or no longer cares what's going on with you. These are fear-generated lies, and they are toxic. Learn to recognize and reject them the moment you hear them.

Fear does not have to have its way with you. Just take God's truth, which will remove fear's power. The truth is that "God has not given us a spirit of fear and timidity, but of power, love, and self-discipline" (2 Tim. 1:7). Fear is not from God. Therefore, there is no reason to believe what fear is trying to tell you! Stand against it with the sword of the Spirit, which is the Word of God (Eph. 6:17). Let it refute every lie and vanquish it from your heart. Learn to recognize the enemy's scent, which is fear. Know that fear always signals his presence. Then refuse to verbalize whatever fear-causing thought he brings to your attention. Camp out in God's perfect love and refuse to budge. God's "love will never invoke fear. Perfect love expels fear, particularly the fear of punishment. The one who fears punishment has not been completed through love" (1 John 4:18 VOICE).

Give the Holy Spirit control over your mind. Remind yourself aloud that your mind belongs to Jesus Christ. Just as you exercise discipline over your bodily health (by eating right, working out, and brushing your teeth), be disciplined in feeding your mind and emotions with God's cleansing truth. Take courage by praying. Repent for entertaining and nurturing fear, or even regarding it as a choice. Reject and renounce it and cast it away from you. Invite the Holy Spirit to minister to you according to the truth and the perfect love of the Father. Invite and embrace the courage God gives!

Live and Learn

- What is the greatest source of discouragement for you in this season, and how has it colored your life? Have you owned these feelings, or are you keeping your discouragement under wraps? How might being more open about your discouragement rob it of its power?

- When you read about Moses being discouraged, does it cause you to view him in a particular light? How does that affect the way you see any discouragement that you are experiencing or have experienced in the past? What adjustments can you make to restore the courage you were created to embrace?

- Where is fear showing up in your life? How has its toxicity affected your emotions and outcomes? What are the specific lies that fear is generating in your life? What truths from God's Word serve to neutralize those lies?

6

FREEDOM IN FORGIVENESS, HEALING IN HUMILITY

———◆———

An angry person starts fights; a hot-tempered person commits all kinds of sin. Pride ends in humiliation, while humility brings honor.

—Proverbs 29:22–23

You never know what tomorrow holds. I'm not a fatalist, and I don't live in dread fear of what tomorrow might bring. But I understand that big, unexpected changes can come suddenly. I don't know what caused the stitches around my pituitary gland to burst and release the blood flow that destroyed my optic nerve. I only know that the pressure on those stitches was too great. I don't know whether anything could have been done differently, and I doubt that my neurosurgeon knows for certain. Suffice to say that *something* went wrong.

Long after my medical crises had passed, one of my daughters shared a memory from those dangerous days. Her words were painful to hear. She simply said, "We didn't know if you were going to wake up, *ever.*"

As a mother, it hurts to think about what my children experienced. I'd lost my own mother a few years earlier, and I remembered watching her slip away. Now my daughter was describing the sense that I might do the same. "They told us that some unconscious patients can hear what's going on around them," she said, "so I leaned in close and whispered in your ear, 'You can't go yet. I'm not ready!'"

How I wish that my family could have been spared all that stress. I also wish that I still had sight in both eyes. But what happened *happened*. There is no going back to my pre-surgery days. I don't say that for the sake of pity or sympathy. I'm not looking to live "under the circumstances" or in the shadow of my past adversity. My prayer is that you won't live there either. My hope is for you to discover forgiveness as the only path forward. There is a blessed humility that comes from trusting the God who allowed your difficulty. And when you humbly release those who seem deserving of punishment, you also set yourself free.

Setting the Record Straight

You don't need anyone to tell you that forgiveness will cost you something. That "something" is your need to punish the person who harmed you. Whatever injury or injustice you suffered, forgiving means payback is no longer an option. That is the Jesus way of doing things. He could have punished us for our sin, but He forgave and redeemed us, at the cost of His life. At the height of His suffering, when He could have despised or even destroyed His tormentors, He said, "Father, *forgive them*, for they don't know what they are doing" (Luke 23:34).

Jesus showed us that forgiveness is a gift, and we are to share it no matter how big a debt we are owed. Without forgiveness, our sin would consume us. Our anger would control us. Insomnia would plague us. Our judgments against others would entrap us. And we would live in resentment and bitterness, terrified that our worst experiences will repeat themselves again and again. No wonder Jesus forgave us and commanded us to forgive others!

To obey Jesus' command, we need to understand what scriptural forgiveness looks like. Many people see it as a religious obligation, a way of managing transgressions that are "small enough" to handle. But the opposite is true! Forgiveness enables us to deal with issues that are far too big to manage or justify. We can't tuck them out of sight and pretend that nothing happened. We need to face them, God's way. He knows how we feel when someone wrongs us. He hears us when we mutter, "But, Lord, that person doesn't deserve forgiveness!"

Some offenses seem unforgivable, but unless we forgive, we cannot be free. If we see forgiveness incorrectly or are unsure what it means, we are less likely to give or receive it. If we mistakenly believe that it means "just getting over it," something inside us will scream, "No! That's not quite right!" Likewise, if we minimize the wrong that was done and tell ourselves, "It's no big deal," we deprive ourselves and our debtors of what forgiveness is designed to do. Denying or downplaying the offense is not forgiveness. It's a big, fat lie! And it heaps on us more emotional baggage than the original injury could.

Years ago, I struggled with something that seemed too big to forgive. I wanted to break free from the emotional mess but could not find the "forgiveness button" anywhere. Then the Lord showed me, not a button to push, but a real way forward. All these years later, I'm still on that journey; but nothing He has shown me has failed me yet. I have been privileged to share it in biblical counseling sessions, in pastoral counseling, and with loved ones. I have seen people suddenly released from years of anguish. Many did not realize that their distress was linked to unforgiveness. Because some of them had not consciously thought about the issue for years, they assumed that they had forgiven their offenders and moved on. That was rarely the case, however.

What I learned is found in Matthew chapter 18, beginning with Peter's question to Jesus: "Lord, how often should I forgive someone who sins against me? Seven times?" (Matt. 18:21). Apparently, Peter believed that a certain amount of forgiveness was enough. We might believe that too, but Jesus doesn't. Listen to what He told Peter: "No, not seven times ... but seventy times seven!" (Matt. 18:22).

The numbers Jesus used were symbolic. Seven represents completion. Seventy times seven was Jesus' way of moving His disciples past the idea of completion, to a lifestyle of forgiveness. He made it clear that forgiveness isn't a numerical formula and those who offer scriptural forgiveness don't keep score. They make forgiveness a way of life. His answer baffled His disciples. So He continued with a story that provides a kind of scriptural blueprint of forgiveness. Let's take it step by step.

> *The Kingdom of Heaven can be compared to a king who decided to bring his accounts up to date with servants who had borrowed money from him (Matthew 18:23).*

The King James Version says the king "would take account" of his debtors (who represent you and me). In other words, before he could forgive, the king (who represents Jesus) had to open his books and note any debts that were still outstanding. That is the first step in forgiving. You acknowledge that someone owes you because of a wrong done. You are not called to deny or diminish the debt but to admit that it exists.

The second step goes a bit further: it is to understand the extent of the loss you suffered. In Jesus' story, the debt owed to the king was astronomical, and some type of repayment had to be arranged.

> *In the process [of reckoning the king's accounts], one of his debtors was brought in who owed him millions of dollars. He couldn't pay, so his master ordered that he be sold—along with his wife, his children, and*

everything he owned—to pay the debt (Matthew 18:24–25).

My study Bible estimates that the man owed the king $52,580,000![5] First and foremost, the enormity of the debt reminds me of my massive debt of sin. But the fact that Jesus used a financial analogy also helps me to grasp the accounting process where forgiveness is concerned. I find that by accounting for the emotional, physical, financial, and relational costs of other people's actions, I know exactly what I am to forgive. For example, how could I be sure that I had forgiven my medical team unless I first recognized everything I lost and could no longer do? I had to open the books and take account. I didn't need a spreadsheet or a ledger book. A simple list was sufficient.

In the story from Matthew 18, the debt was so great that repayment could only be addressed by selling the debtor, his family, and his goods. Whether that was enough to cover what the king actually lost, I don't know. But that was all the servant had to offer, and the thought of it terrified him. So he did what anyone in his shoes would do:

> *The man fell down before his master and begged him, "Please, be patient with me, and I will pay it all." Then his master was filled with pity for him, and he released him and forgave his debt (Matthew 18:26–27).*

The third step in the process is for the offended party to offer mercy and redemption. At great cost to himself, the king released his servant and forgave every penny of his debt. That is what God did for us. We could not pay our debt of sin. So, through Adam and Eve, we were sold to the devil until the ransom payment of the cross could be made. It was the ultimate price, and Jesus paid it willingly. When His work was finished, our redemption was sealed. Our debt was cleared from the books.

When someone causes us harm, we need to remember how Jesus responded to our sin. Those who hurt us need the same mercy and forgiveness that we have received. Even if they recognize what their actions have cost us, they are incapable of making restitution. My neurosurgeon, his assistants, nurses, and others involved with the stitches in my brain did not mean to injure me. But their intent is not the issue. What I lost is priceless. No one could possibly compensate me for it. The only scriptural way forward was for me to show mercy and forgive anyone and everyone who might be culpable for the outcome of my first brain surgery.

In financial realms, a forgiven debt is purged from the books. That means repayment is no longer expected. Likewise, when I chose to forgive, I released all parties from any responsibility to make restitution. Regardless of what I lost or suffered, I had to cancel the debt and mark it "Paid in Full."

That is the cost of forgiveness. But there is also a reward. As long as you expect repayment, you are bound to the person you hold responsible for your trouble. When you drop this expectation, you sever that connection. This is where restoration begins! Instead of focusing on the one who hurt you, you look to the only One who is able to restore even your hope.

The servant in Matthew 18 experienced a glorious turnaround and seemed destined for better days. The king cleared his path forward and set him completely free. But the man was unwilling to drop his expectations of repayment where others were concerned. After being forgiven of his extreme debt, he tormented someone who owed him a miniscule sum. The king was infuriated.

Then the king called in the man he had forgiven and said, "You evil servant! I forgave you that tremendous debt because you pleaded with me. Shouldn't you have mercy on your fellow servant, just as I had mercy on you?" Then the angry king sent the man to prison to be tortured until he had paid his entire debt (Matthew 18:32–34).

If we refuse to forgive others, we will be delivered to the torment of reliving the anguish we suffered when they hurt us. The longer we resist the call to forgiveness, the more deeply the torment will scar our hearts, darken our outlook, and corrupt the workings of the subconscious mind. That is the terrible price of unforgiveness.

BEING HUMBLED IS HEALING

Whether we are on the giving or receiving end of it, forgiveness is humbling. So is knowing that God purposefully tests us at times, not to punish us or cut us down to size, but because He is actively and lovingly involved in our development. We sometimes think we know everything we need to know about our issues, but our Father knows that is not true. In His mercy, He helps us to recognize it.

The tests that God allows are reality checks, and they often happen during periods of trouble or transition. When God delivered the Israelites from Pharaoh's grip, they did not expect their newfound freedom to humble them, especially knowing that God Himself had freed them. But the journey tested them. One test came when they realized that their customary diet was not on the wilderness menu. So they complained to Moses and even accused him of trying to starve them to death (Exod. 16:1–3). God addressed their agitation with a plan only He could devise.

Look, I'm going to rain down food from heaven for you. Each day the people can go out and pick up as much food as they need for that day. I will test them in this to see whether or not they will follow my instructions. On the sixth day they will gather food, and when they prepare it, there will be twice as much as usual (Exodus 16:4–5).

What God promised was an exquisite form of provision. But as Moses explained later, the giving of manna was also a test.

He fed you with manna in the wilderness, a food unknown to your ancestors. He did this to humble you and test you for your own good. (Deuteronomy 8:16).

God tested the Israelites in order to humble them. That they needed to be humbled seems counterintuitive. After all, they had been brutally subjugated in Egypt for hundreds of years. Yet even after being downtrodden, they were vulnerable to pride. Perhaps because God had arranged their wilderness journey, they expected Him to provide for them. In fact, they came to see manna as their right. When God rained down nourishment from heaven, it did not meet their standards, so they as much as said, "If You are going to supernaturally provide for us anyway, why not give us something tasty to eat?"

At some point, all of us complain to God when we should be brimming with gratitude. Like the Israelites, we sometimes grouse about His goodness! That is how the Israelites failed God's test. Their reaction to the manna revealed whether they were humble enough to admit they needed God, or whether they saw Egypt or even themselves as their provider.

We naturally tend toward proving our independence and taking credit for our accomplishments. We also crave the freedom to choose what we do, where we live, and what we eat.

We don't like being dependent on others, because it limits our choices. This is exactly why the manna was about more than provision. It tested the Israelites' attitude toward their dependency on God. It also revealed their sense that He was withholding what they "deserved" to have.

Friends, when life gets really difficult, don't jump to the conclusion that God isn't on the job. Instead, be glad that you are in the very thick of what Christ experienced. This is a spiritual refining process, with glory just around the corner (1 Peter 4:12–13 MSG).

Have you ever chafed under God's provision, as the Israelites did? Did He "fail" to answer your prayers in the way you expected? Did He enable you to buy a house that was less than the dream home you envisioned? Did you thank Him for sending you a spouse and decide later that His provision no longer met your standards? Do you believe that you could have made a better choice on your own?

We need to ask ourselves whether we are we grateful, or only grateful under certain conditions. Do we realize that God is testing and humbling us? Are we ready to embrace the test and the humility it brings? I had to ask myself these questions many times (and still do). I knew that my heavenly Father was providing well for me. During the period when I could not drive, I never lacked for transportation. But would I have remained grateful if I had not been able to get behind the wheel again? Would I be content in my dependency and thankful to be alive, even if I had to rely on others for the rest of my life? Or would I have carped about not having it "my way"?

God's tests are not designed to exasperate us. He tests us in order to equip us. As I write, the entire world is being tested by a virus and its terrible effects. Will we allow even this test to teach us? Are we willing to admit that we are still in the process of maturing? Can we humble ourselves before God and others? Are we willing to forgive them as Christ forgave us?

May our seasons of adversity increase our humility and incline us to forgive more each day. May the softening of our hearts make us stronger, more compassionate, and better able to love and obey our God, for He is worthy!

LIVE AND LEARN

- How do you respond when someone else's actions make it impossible to return to what "used to be"? How can you reconcile yourself to the fact that your life was changed without your permission? What is the hardest part about letting go of the desire to punish? What will help you to let go?

- Have you ever struggled with forgiveness because you thought it meant ignoring the damage someone did? How did that struggle end up, and how do you see forgiveness differently now? How, specifically, might having a sound biblical view of forgiveness (1) free you from the weight of past losses, and (2) help you to deal with a current situation?

- Describe how the need for more humility is showing up in a specific situation in your life. How might you be helped by knowing that God allowed the situation? How did your view of life's tests affect your response to a past situation? Has God failed to meet your expectations? How so? What does your answer reveal (1) about God, and (2) about your perspective?

7

COUNTERCULTURAL
OBEDIENCE

———◆———

*Do you think all God wants are sacrifices—empty
rituals just for show? He wants you to listen to him!
Plain listening is the thing, not staging a lavish religious production.*

—*1 Samuel 15:22 MSG*

When the title of your message includes the word *obedience*,
you can expect some furrowed brows and crossed arms.
The very mention of the word can make people feel uptight, and
understandably so. The subject is often reduced to a checklist of
things "good Christians" should and should not do. But a life
of obedience is about more than rule-keeping. It is an opportunity to live in a way that is pleasing, not only to God but to you.

For the record, people who choose to obey God are not perfect. They are people—flawed, changeable, and in need of God's
mercy and grace. Although I am very conscious of the choices
I make and eager to please the Lord whose love is seamless, I
am human and prone to human missteps. I am thankful when
I get it right, but sometimes I get it wrong. I managed to do
both during my season of adversity, and the consequences of
my choices are still playing out.

Although much in this life is beyond our control, we have a definite part to play. That was true where my surgical recovery was concerned, and the lesson unfolded in very practical ways. I learned that even when doctors did everything they could do, I had to do certain things myself. One of them was breathing. That sounds obvious, but because of pneumonia and repeated insertions of the breathing tube, taking deep breaths was painful and triggered endless fits of coughing. Those difficult breaths were important to my recovery, but I often took the easier, more shallow breaths that seemed less costly in the short term.

Clearly, they were not enough. As my daughters watched the machines monitoring my physical condition, they begged aloud, "Breathe, Momma! Breathe!"

"I *am* breathing!" I answered in frustration. "If I weren't, I wouldn't be here!"

Naturally, my smart answer didn't work any better than my shallow breaths did. The screen that tracked my vitals didn't care how much it hurt me to breathe. It only cared about how much oxygen I was getting and how well my lungs were working. There was a decision to make, and only I could make it. Either I would cooperate with my recovery, or I would contribute to my demise. If I chose recovery, I would have to push past the pain. I had already agreed with God that I would not die. But agreeing with Him was not enough. To recover fully, I had to back up my agreement with some good old-fashioned obedience. To my family's relief, I did.

I wasn't quite as cooperative in another area, however. During my hospital stay, my voice was compromised and had grown weak. So my medical team recommended voice therapy. The last thing I wanted was to take on another medical regimen. I already had my hands full with physical and occupational therapy, and I was in no hurry to become anyone else's "project." So I assumed that my voice was weak because the ordeal had left *me* weak. I was sure that when I got stronger, my voice would also bounce back, so I refused the therapy.

In retrospect, I let myself off the hook because the idea of more therapy seemed like "too much." I did not properly consider the cause of my voice trouble. Yes, I was physically weak, but that wasn't the reason my voice was failing. There was structural damage from the breathing tube. The tissues that produced my voice needed rehabilitation to minimize the long-term damage. No one was trying to overwhelm me or make me their project. My medical team was offering therapy because I needed it.

My failure to cooperate has been costly. The damage to my voice is consequential to my life and my work as a pastor and teacher. I have to carefully ration my voice and rest it often. It not only sounds different, but using it consumes a great deal of energy that would be better used elsewhere. My refusal to do the therapy was more than a mistake; it was a form of disobedience. God had not audibly commanded me to accept the treatment, and there is no scripture verse that says, "Thou shalt receive voice therapy." But I am certain that my decision was not what God had in mind.

Isaiah 1:19 says, "If you are willing and obedient, you will eat the best from the land" (GW). Obedience goes beyond the letter of the law. To be willing and obedient is to respond to the spirit of the law and to the Lawgiver. Because I was unwilling to accept the treatment I needed, I am not eating "the best from the land" where my voice is concerned. God still loves me and accepts me, but I am living with the consequences of my choice.

THE DISCIPLE'S OBEDIENCE

Obedience is part of being yoked with Jesus, and both decisions are voluntary. The same is true of all that God commands. His expectations are clear, but He gives us the freedom not to meet them. We choose whether we will live authentically and whole-heartedly as His disciples. And if we choose that way of life, it will demand much more of us than lip service. It means willingly and actively obeying Him regardless of any inconvenience, whether or not we fully understand the *why* behind what He requires. Either He is Lord to us, or He isn't. And if He is, there is no question as to whether we should obey Him.

Jesus' perspective on obedience could not be any clearer than what He said in Luke chapter 6:

> *Why do you call Me "Lord, Lord," and not do the things which I say? Whoever comes to Me, and hears My sayings and does them, I will show you whom he is like: He is like a man building a house, who dug deep and laid the foundation on the rock. And when the flood arose, the stream beat vehemently against that house, and could not shake it, for it was founded on the rock. But he who heard and did nothing is like a man who built a house on the earth without a foundation, against which the stream beat vehemently; and immediately it fell. And the ruin of that house was great"* (Luke 6:46–49 NKJV).

It is easy to call Jesus your Lord. Clearly, He is Lord of all! But true discipleship means living like He is *your* Lord. When Jesus talks about hearing His words and doing them, He is talking about more than accepting His teachings in order to join His "group." That kind of corporate acceptance has its place. For example, followers of Christ claim adherence to the Bible, the foundational document of the faith. When we become part of certain Christian fellowships, we know what the church believes as a group. But many Christians have reduced discipleship to conformity and the observance of rules. Please understand that we are absolutely called to obey God's Word. But is obeying Him a matter of checking off the boxes? Is He only concerned with whether or not we appear to honor His teachings?

I don't think so. Hearing Christ's teachings and applying them to our everyday lives are essential. But for His followers, that is just the start of obedience. True discipleship involves a more personal, unbounded willingness to adhere to whatever pleases Him. This kind of spirituality goes beyond a rote sense of religion. It exceeds the mere acceptance of principles and teachings. Instead, it is complete submission to His absolute authority as Lord. This devotion shows up not only in the words of true disciples, but in how they live their lives, day by day.

I am not suggesting a holier-than-thou approach or a class of "super Christians" who believe their group is on a fast track to heaven. The only perfect model of Christlikeness was Christ Himself. The rest of us do our best, learn from our mistakes, and allow Him to change us into His image and likeness. Thankfully, His mercies are new every morning (Lam. 3:22–23). Every day is potentially a day of growth in which we move closer to His intent for us. This is part of the believer's journey—the process that continues for as long as we are blessed to live.

And so, dear brothers and sisters, I plead with you to give your bodies to God because of all he has done for you. Let them be a living and holy sacrifice—the kind he will find acceptable. This is truly the way to worship him (Romans 12:1).

BECOMING COUNTERCULTURAL

The idea of unquestioned obedience to God is unpopular in secular Western culture. At best, it is seen as an antiquated way of living; at worst, it is deemed foolish. The reason, in my opinion, is that many people judge obedience apart from the One to whom we render it. Without a sense of the God we worship, obeying Him seems hollow, and all obedience looks like blind obedience, which is unsound. So the baby (unquestioned obedience to God) gets thrown out with the bathwater (blind obedience to an idea), and the culture flounders.

What we desperately need is to reconnect our obedience to the One who is worthy of it. He is not only the One we obey; He is the reason we obey. Our obedience is part of our worship. Therefore, it is not a method for being blessed. Of course, the Bible describes many people who were blessed in their obedience—people like Abraham, Hannah, Mary of Bethany, and more. They were willing and obedient, and they enjoyed God's best. However, their obedience was the fruit of their worship.

Despite the Bible's clear-cut case, obedience is not widely cultivated in our culture or even in parts of Christ's church! Instead, some leaders stress the faith for blessing, as though blessing could be assured apart from obedience. Until it is combined with obedience, faith is little more than a gesture. Believing is essential, but blessing does not come simply because we have faith for it. Blessing grows in the fertile soil of obedience. Expecting one without the other is like wrestling with God in the hope of bending His will to ours. That is a match we will lose every time!

Another common misunderstanding is the idea that compliance and obedience are the same thing. They are not. Genuine obedience rests in the believer's willingness to do whatever God requires. Compliance is often disguised as obedience, but the compliant person goes through the motions with no buy-in and no sense of having any other choice. It is more of a default position than a proactive choice. People who truly obey God are not defaulting; they are motivated to love, honor, and respect Him as their Lord. Their obedience comes from the heart and demonstrates their active trust in Him. They obey Him because

He is worthy, and they consciously make godly choices regardless of the inconvenience it might cause. That kind of obedience is countercultural.

It is also Christlike. In the garden of Gethsemane, Jesus asked whether the Father might remove the cup Jesus was about to drink. The Father did not remove it, and Jesus did not question the decision. Instead, He arose from prayer in what seemed like a completely different frame of mind from the one that prompted His question. He did not act like someone in dread fear of the suffering ahead. He stood up from His prayer time courageous, willing, and determined to complete the work He was sent to accomplish.

Jesus knew what His obedience would cost Him. Yet He agreed to pay the price, because His love and trust in His heavenly Father were complete. These qualities, combined with His nature as God in the flesh, made Him the perfect intermediary between God and humankind. Personal gain did not motivate Jesus. He was willing to do what Peter thought was detrimental, and He was willing to suffer more than any human being ever had and ever would. And He did it with one motive in mind: to accomplish His Father's desire.

In a culture that devalues obedience, the thought of guaranteed pain and suffering is not a selling point! For millions of Christians, pain and suffering are signs that one's faith has failed. Beloved, this is a terrible misunderstanding of the truth. There is no reproach or shame in suffering that is born of obedience to God. Quite the contrary! The suffering of obedience leads to blessing for you and for the plan of God. That idea is countercultural, and it glorifies God.

WHEN OBEDIENCE LOOKS WRONG

Don't fret when your obedience causes people to scratch their heads. The things you do for His sake might seem crazy and make them wonder whether you're a little "off." Show them some mercy! They misunderstand you because they cannot see beyond the surface of your actions. They only know that what you are doing doesn't overtly serve your immediate interests. They can't understand why you pay your tithes when money is tight. In fact, they don't understand why you pay them at all! They are dumbfounded when you don't retaliate for their unkindness, even when they clearly did you wrong. Have compassion for them and pray for them to catch glimpses of how God sees these things. (Someone probably prayed that way for you at some point!) Be content in knowing that "the 'foolish' things of God have proven to be wiser than human wisdom. And the 'feeble' things of God have proven to be far more powerful than any human ability" (1 Cor. 1:25 TPT).

At times, your choices might look like anything but obedience to those who are watching. Being misunderstood in this way is humbling. If you would rather protect your name than be misunderstood, you might be tempted to surrender to peer pressure. You might even comply with your detractors' mistaken ideas of what is right. This temptation has perhaps never been more common than it is today, when the things the world calls *good* and *right* are the very things that God despises.

Jesus experienced this kind of conflict during His earthly walk. The religious role models of His day questioned what they saw as His unorthodox approach to life and faith. They even questioned His identity. Nazarenes saw Him as a carpenter's son, and an illegitimate one at that. They knew He was conceived before Joseph and Mary were officially married. And if that was not offensive enough, He claimed to be the completely legitimate Son of God. Imagine their outrage when He tested the worldview that underpinned their position and power!

Yet Jesus never tried to prove His legitimacy. He just continued doing what His Father sent Him to do. More often than not, His actions ruffled feathers and raised the fury of the self-righteous. To them, His obedience seemed outright sinful. But He never allowed their accusations to bait Him, and He never caved under their pressure.

Even the devil himself could not tempt Jesus to prove Himself. When His physical weakness from fasting was at its peak, the devil taunted Him, saying, "How can you possibly be the Son of God and go hungry? Just command these stones to be turned into loaves of bread" (Matt. 4:3 TPT). When Jesus refused, the devil goaded Him to prove God's Word by throwing Himself from the highest point of the temple. The devil said, "If you're really God's Son, jump, and the angels will catch you. For it is written in the Scriptures: He will command his angels to protect you and they will lift you up so that you won't even bruise your foot on a rock" (Matt. 4:6 TPT).

In our human nature, we want to prove ourselves when people misunderstand or resent us. Jesus did not fall into that trap. He knew that His unique standing as fully man and fully God would stir controversy, but He felt no need to prove His credentials to the devil or anyone else. Jesus knew who He was! (Truth be told, so did Satan and all his cohorts.) He simply accepted being misunderstood and maligned.

In His obedience to the Father, Jesus sometimes said things that defied the custom. Therefore, many saw His words as deviations from social and religious norms. For example, when an unnamed disciple wanted to follow Jesus after first burying his father, Jesus said, "Follow me now. Let the spiritually dead bury their own dead" (Matt. 8:22). To many in the crowd, Jesus' response sounded disrespectful and culturally inappropriate. Tending to family was the honorable thing to do, and it still is. But their perspective was incomplete. Jesus was not minimizing devotion to family. He was speaking to a larger and deeper issue that tested the motives of the man's heart. Jesus encouraged him to do that which would give him life. This boggled the man's mind. To understand it would require him to recognize how his natural perspectives were clouding his vision and even holding him hostage. If he allowed Jesus' invitation to free him, he would have to rethink his views of right and wrong.

Peter learned a similar lesson when Jesus told the disciples that He was going to Jerusalem, where He would die. To Peter, the idea was absurd, if not suicidal. The thought that his Messiah would submit Himself to suffering infuriated Peter. So he "took [Jesus] aside and began to reprimand him for saying such things. 'Heaven forbid, Lord,' he said. 'This will never happen to you!' Jesus turned to Peter and said, 'Get away from me, Satan! You are a dangerous trap to me. You are seeing things merely from a human point of view, not from God's'" (Matt. 16:22–23).

Jesus knew what He was doing: He was proceeding in obedience to the divine plan, which included dying on the cross. The idea shocked Peter. Jesus' sharp response must have shocked him even more. Peter thought his desire to protect Jesus was both good and caring, and from a natural perspective, it was. But Jesus' response showed that Peter's view was far from the divine perspective.

We can fault Peter, but we are susceptible to the same tendencies he was. We have certain ideas about how obedience should look. Sometimes we get it right; but some of what we believe reveals our misunderstanding of what God desires, especially when suffering is involved. Jesus did not comply with Peter's preconceptions of how the Messiah was supposed to act, and He will not comply with ours. He is not fazed by natural, human perspectives, and His ways will shatter our myths about God. Just look at what He told His disciples:

> *Don't imagine that I came to bring peace to the earth! I came not to bring peace, but a sword. "I have come to set a man against his father, a daughter against her mother, and a daughter-in-law against her mother-in-law. Your enemies will be right in your own*

household!" If you love your father or mother more
than you love me, you are not worthy of being mine;
or if you love your son or daughter more than me, you
are not worthy of being mine (Matthew 10:34–37).

Jesus' words seem completely contrary to people's expectations of what the Messiah would say. They certainly challenge our cultural version of Christianity. After all, shouldn't belief in the Prince of Peace produce peace all around us, and especially in our own families? If we think one-dimensionally, the answer is *yes*. But God's view is more expanded than that. Obedience to His will does not always look the way we expect it to.

If Jesus' obedience was not a crowd-pleaser, our obedience might not satisfy public opinion either. Our role is simply to see as God sees and obey Him. We are not called to please people. We are called to serve our King.

A Clear Mandate to Obey

As we walk with God and are led by His Spirit, our obedience will ruffle feathers, including our own. I am not advocating bizarre behaviors that masquerade as the leading of the Spirit. I am saying that our obedience won't always line up with the world's view of what is right. It might not even agree with our family's ideas. Stepping outside the perspectives that are considered normal will surely test our mettle. In the end, we will find out whether we are going through the motions and offering lip service or walking in personal obedience to God.

It is time. We are called to stand out from the culture by cultivating the soil of obedience and tearing up the fallow ground of conformity and peer pressure. The Lord God is worthy of our complete and total trust. Jesus' ultimate act of obedience was rooted in His trust and love for His Father. The more we trust and love Him, the more likely we are to obey Him. And the more we obey, the more our trust and love of Him will increase.

As was true of the resurrection that followed Jesus' suffering, something more profound and life-giving awaits us on the other side of our obedience. Let's choose obedience with joy—not fearing the cost but embracing the call. Whatever the cost might be, the fruit of our obedience will be greater. In all of it, we can be thankful!

Live and Learn

- Because you are human, there can be gaps between your "Lord, Lord," and your unquestioned obedience. In what specific area do gaps show up most often? What is hindering your willingness to obey? Is it the fear of where your obedience will lead? Or might you be unwilling (so far) to break with a certain custom that seems right? Explain.

- Can you see in your own life examples of when your obedience moved beyond a basic adherence to Jesus' teaching and embraced His guidance on a more personal level? What sets these experiences apart from others? Where are you currently being stretched along these lines? How might facing the challenge draw you closer to Jesus?

- Based on the idea that obedience to God can look like disobedience to the world, how might you have misjudged the choices of a Christian brother or sister? What about that situation tripped you up? How do you see it differently now, and how might this new perspective guide your own choices in the future?

8

THE ATTITUDE OF THANKFULNESS

———◆———

Enter his gates with thanksgiving; go into his courts
with praise. Give thanks to him and praise his name.
—Psalms 100:4

E ven if you never laid eyes on a Bible, you would probably
appreciate the importance of gratitude. Most parents do
a great job of teaching their children to say "thank you" when
someone shows them kindness. In fact, the lesson can become
second nature. But like all good habits, it can slip into formality,
like saying "I'm fine" when someone asks how you are. When
habit takes over or obligation motivates your responses, you can
say the right words but miss the point. When you do this with
God, you can forget to say, "Thank You, Lord, for giving me life
and loving me in spite of myself!"

Life is loaded with distractions, so staying thankful requires
intentionality. When everything seems to be going your way,
you can become accustomed to it and forget the One who
helped and still cares for you. You can also lose touch with your
gratitude in seasons of adversity. The enemy of your soul will try
to convince you that God doesn't care. If you stay focused on the
truth, you will reject that lie, and your season of adversity—the

time when your very existence seems to be on the line—will cause you to give thanks for every little thing that goes right.

If you have been there, you know what I mean. When you can't pay your bills or fill your cupboard, finding a ten-dollar bill in an old coat pocket can make you dance! And when a tornado reduces your house to matchsticks, finding an old photo album in the rubble can bring you to your knees.

That was more or less how I felt when the doctor told us that I would not be intubated again. It was a *very* big deal! Thankfulness coursed through my being like a rushing river of joy. I had not failed to appreciate the benefits of the breathing tube, but the tube had done its work. I was thrilled to be separated from it and the complications that came with it. If I live to be a hundred and twenty, I might never adequately describe how ecstatic I was over what the Lord did that day. I pray that you and I both live in that kind of joy *every* day! Really, we can, and almost nothing will get us there like thankfulness will.

THANKFULNESS IS A KEY

Usually, we are thankful in response to something that touches us. But thankfulness is not only for life's grand moments. We can give thanks when our excitement about God's goodness seems buried under layers of grief or sorrow. In those seasons, our hearts want to complain about His timing or seeming absence. In our frustration, we tend to withhold our gratitude, like pouting children who are so used to getting their way that they expect to win all the time. In our adversity, we can we lose sight of God and all that He is doing behind the scenes. Without realizing it, we stop living and find ourselves going through the motions. We let life's demands carry us along, and we lose sight of its wonders.

We don't have to live that way! Whatever we face, and however battered our lives and hearts might be, we can give thanks to God for every breath. He is worthy of our praise, not because life is perfect, but because He is God. Therefore, we can be thankful in whatever imperfect state we find ourselves. In fact, God's Word commands us to be thankful.

Our gratitude is more than a "law," however. It is also a key to our communion with God.

Our heavenly Father invites us into His presence and welcomes us into His throne room, not because He needs us to come, but because He knows what we need. So He gives us a key to His heavenly dwelling place and invites us to let ourselves in anytime.

As a parent, I can totally relate to that! Harvey and I love when our kids come over. We know they are grown adults, but when they stop by, it feels like they've come home. We are so happy to see them, and we delight in their presence. They have their own homes and families, but we want them to know that our home is still theirs. So we gave each of them their own keys and the code to our garage door. Whether Harvey and I are at home or away, our children are free to come and go as they please.

The God-given key of thankfulness works in a similar way: it shows us that our heavenly Father welcomes us to feel at home with Him. In fact, He loves having us around! So when the psalm says, "Enter his gates with thanksgiving; go into his courts with praise," I see God handing me a very large key that will throw open His gates. I know that if I offer my praise, it will lead me directly into His courts, where I will commune with Him.

Friend, we can know these things, and we can *know* them. When we read the Scriptures—especially the ones that are most familiar—we sometimes brush over the details and assume they are unrelated to our modern-day experiences. But biblical ideas are timeless and forever relevant. We just need to *see* what they mean to us. Because of the work Harvey and I do in Africa, words like *gates* and *courts* are very relatable and make the picture of thankfulness more real to us. Most of the places we stay in Africa have gates and courts. The gate is only entryway, and it is set in a high wall that wraps around the entire compound. Once you pass through the gate, you can see living spaces arranged around a central courtyard where people congregate for fellowship, meals, and entertainment. It is also where the children play.

These memories help me to see what God means when He invites me into His gates and courts. When I enter, I have a sense that I am coming home! The place is welcoming, and I feel safe and totally accepted. Intimacy and community exist together, and with my family in Christ, I enjoy a sense of both knowing and being known. It is beautiful!

My heavenly key not only opens the gates, but it transports me there in an instant! I don't have to drive for days or hop on a plane. I can reach my Father's dwelling place the moment I make the choice to visit. There are no scheduling conflicts or restricted hours. There are no waiting lines, and no preapproval is needed. As long as I use my key, I have immediate access to God's house from anyplace, at any time!

When adversity strikes, my key seems even more precious to me, and I feel an even greater need to be where I am safe and always welcome. Yet when trouble begins to grind me down, I can lose sight of my key. I can misplace my gratitude and struggle to get into His presence—when I need Him the most. Even when I keep praying, I can feel as though the heavens have closed and no help is coming.

Friend, all of us have had those moments, but I know this: that feeling is a lie from hell itself. When you embrace it, you get cranky with God and everyone else. You can even believe that everyone is conspiring against you. As though your circumstances weren't difficult enough, you can develop a disturbing attitude to go with them! Doing this is like locking yourself out of the safe haven you desperately want and need to enter.

Instead of finding respite, you pile on more layers of frustration and dig yourself a deeper pit of pain.

If you have been there or are there right now, don't stay there! God has not locked you out. Just reach for your key and use it! Let the heart of thanksgiving transport you home and open His gates. Love and acceptance await you there.

Thankfulness Is an Attitude

The thanksgiving key is part of our heritage in God. The Old Testament psalmists understood it, and so did the original apostles. Paul wrote this about it: "Be cheerful no matter what; pray all the time; thank God no matter what happens. This is the way God wants you who belong to Christ Jesus to live." (1 Thess. 5:18 MSG).

Notice how Paul emphasizes using your key "in every situation … continually." He wanted the church at Thessalonica (and us) to understand how important it is to give God thanks. Paul made it clear that thankfulness is more than a feeling or a polite knock on heaven's door. And it is certainly more than lip service to God. You can mouth words that sound thankful while you're stewing in a sour attitude. The words will sound right, but they won't conceal your inner conflict from Him.

The key that God gave you works perfectly when it is used faithfully. Thankfulness is not a one-dimensional feeling or action. The giving of thanks is much bigger than that: it is an attitude that underpins your feelings and "doings." This is significant, because attitudes don't just happen; you choose them. Whether your circumstances are trying or totally wonderful, you still get to choose how you feel about them. Difficult circumstances don't force you to whine or be ungrateful any more than smooth sailing forces you to be content. Your attitude is always your decision.

Thankfulness is a moment-by-moment choice. God provided the key, but only you can use it. If you want to be where you are loved, welcomed, accepted, refreshed, and strengthened, use your key! Express your gratitude to Him and the gates will swing open. And because His goodness has no end, the more thanks you give, the more things you will find to be thankful for! So by choosing to be grateful, you perpetuate your attitude of gratitude.

That is exactly what Paul was getting at: if you choose to be thankful, you can come and go into your heavenly safe haven at will—not just when you feel thankful, but when you choose to come despite your feelings. God is your help, and He is there.

GIVING THANKS IN THE DARK PLACES

When we are surrounded by circumstances we cannot control, Paul's ideas about thankfulness can seem counterintuitive. To the natural mind, God's wisdom *is* counterintuitive. Yet it makes perfect sense. Consider what Paul did *not* say: he did not say to give thanks *for* life's sorrows and catastrophes. That would be absurd and akin to blaming God for them. Not everything that happens in our lives comes from God. Some things happen because the enemy is a thief, and his "purpose is to steal and kill and destroy" (John 10:10). Other troubles result from what we have wrought in our flesh nature, whether through ignorance or willfulness.

Paul said to give thanks *in* our hardships—not just so God will rescue us, but because we worship Him regardless of how things turn out. When we maintain this attitude in every situation, we open ourselves to God's involvement and remind ourselves that no matter what is happening, we have reason to be thankful. Why? Because Jesus is there! He promised never to leave or forsake us (Heb. 13:5), and His promises are never empty. Whatever turmoil we experience, Jesus is right there with us. He is worthy of our gratitude!

> *Come, let us sing to the LORD! Let us shout joyfully to the Rock of our salvation. Let us come to him with thanksgiving. Let us sing psalms of praise to him. For the LORD is a great God, a great King above all gods (Psalms 95:1-3).*

When you keep your eyes on Jesus and learn to see your situation as He does, giving thanks comes naturally, even in adversity. But if you have misplaced your thankfulness in the whirlwind of your suffering, take a moment to pause and count your blessings. Remind yourself of how much better off you are because Jesus is with you. When chaos surrounds you, imagine how much worse off you would be without Him!

Jesus' love for you is unequaled. Your spouse might love you to the moon and back, and your children might smother you in kisses, but no one can love you like Jesus loves you—not even you. He cares for you better than you can care for yourself. Your knowledge and resources are finite, but His are unlimited. No detail of your situation is beyond His understanding, provision, or power. You might feel overwhelmed by the complexities you are facing, but He is not. He knew about it long before you did. When you have no clue about how to proceed, He knows the perfect way through. In fact, He has a plan in mind and provision in place to see His plan to completion.

Remember what God's Word says: "We know that God causes everything to work together for the good of those who love God and are called according to his purpose for them" (Rom 8:28).

Those words bear repeating—and often! Regardless of how massive your problem seems to be, you will come out of it with something good. No matter what the enemy has up his sleeve, God's plan for good is unshakeable. So when your world quakes, keep standing. Focus on what you know about His goodness, and your faith will be strengthened. The more consistent your focus becomes, the more aware you will be of your need for Him, and the more open you will be to His involvement.

Let this awareness help you to see His plan more clearly. Then cooperate with it and watch what happens! The more you cooperate, the more you will find yourself thanking Him— not only for His power, but for His willingness to use it on your behalf.

RECONDITIONING YOUR HEART

When you thank your heavenly Father, your heart toward Him is softened. The softer your heart becomes, the less prone you are to fear and anxiety. So tell Him, "Thank You for reminding me through Your Word that all things work together for my good. Thank You for reminding me that You will never leave me. Thank You for knowing about this situation before I had any clue it was coming. And thank You for making provision ahead of time. Thank You, Lord, for Your plan and for leading me through this trial with Your love!"

Consistently acknowledging these realities and thanking God for them changes your heart and your outlook. In fact, it is one way of guarding your heart, as Scripture commands. This is important, because "everything you do flows from it" (Prov. 4:23 NIV). In other words, *everything* that flows from your heart reflects its condition and affects your life. Guarding it is critical! You don't guard your heart the same way you guard a bank, however. You don't protect your heart by putting a wall around it. Instead, you guard your heart by keeping it open to God. And the more open-hearted you are toward Him, the more your heart is closed to demonic oppression and the world's ways of fear and worry.

A guarded heart is a tender heart. The more tender your heart is toward God, the better able you are to receive from Him the things you need. If you lack thankfulness, you will inadvertently refuse the goodness, wisdom, strength, and peace you need. An unguarded heart is plagued by bitterness, resentment, anger, judgmentalism, accusation, negativity, hopelessness, and unforgiveness, and it responds to negative circumstances in self-sabotaging ways. You might beg God for deliverance yet find yourself resisting Him. Worst of all, you can be tricked into believing that He is ignoring your cries for help. If you believe that, you will almost surely make unwise decisions and cause yourself unnecessary complications and anguish.

Much of life is beyond your control, but you always have control over your own heart. Owning that fact is so important, because the condition of your heart determines whether you come into agreement with God, your flesh, or the devil. Your agreement may or may not be consciously decided, but it will affect you and determine your relationship to God's promises. For example, Jesus said that He came to give life and life more abundantly (John 10:10). But unless you are walking in agreement with Him, you will experience little of that abundance. Only a tenderized heart can cooperate with Jesus and see His promises fulfilled.

The message of this chapter is so simple that you can miss its application to your complicated circumstances. Yet it applies, and in powerful ways! Godly gratitude is a key, and anyone who wants to use it can do so. If you will seek God's face, guard your heart, and remain thankful, you will turn the key that He has given you. That decision will lead you toward the very thing you are asking of Him. And when nothing in life seems certain, you will carry on, with joy and in peace!

Live and Learn

- Can you remember a time when persistent abundance or persistent lack took the edge off your sense of thankfulness to God? How did that affect your heart and life? Did a deep, abiding gratitude return? If so, what caused the change? If not, how might you regain it?

- How does the idea of thankfulness as a God-given key to His throne room affect your outlook where seasons of difficulty are concerned? What does receiving such a key tell you about how God cares for you? If you are a parent, what about God's approach speaks to you the most? As a child in the natural sense, how does this idea remind you of a way in which your parent(s) or guardian(s) made you feel at home, or failed to do so?

- How does your overall demeanor most reflect an attitude of thankfulness? In what ways does it least reflect thankfulness? What, in your mind, is most significant about seeing thankfulness as an attitude rather than an act?

9

PEACE IN UNCERTAINTY

———◆·◆———

I have told you all this so that you may have peace in me. Here on earth you will have many trials and sorrows. But take heart, because I have overcome the world.
—*John 16:33*

Like adversity, uncertainty is a fact of life. Even when your world is running on all cylinders, uncertainty is present. Economies change. Culture changes. History happens. Relationships evolve. We grow older and our bodies change. Some changes are for the better. Others are less welcome. Some changes announce themselves ahead of time. Others explode on the scene without warning. These unforeseen changes seem to threaten our peace the most.

You already know about the unsettled feeling I had when I left the hospital and entered my recovery period. I never saw it coming! It seemed only logical that a stable recovery period would be easier to handle than the sheer chaos I experienced during my hospitalization. So when my peace disappeared, I was dumbstruck.

What I learned was that uncertainty can only steal your peace when something is out of alignment. In my case, the issue was an unspoken confusion about my role and Jesus' role in my recovery. I had assumed responsibility that was not mine to assume and stepped out of alignment where His Lordship was concerned. In that context, uncertainty gained the upper hand and snatched my peace.

For the believer, the absence or disturbance of peace should be a clue that something needs adjusting. We were divinely created as integrated beings, with spirit, soul, and body intertwined and interrelated. When one area is shaken, the disturbance affects other areas. In fact, everything we have covered in this book is connected to everything else. That means getting in the yoke with Jesus is connected to taking courage, and taking courage is connected to obeying Him. Humility and forgiveness are inseparable, and thankfulness is threaded through everything we feel and do. All of these pieces affect how we experience or don't experience peace.

If there is anything we humans want, it is peace! The goal is to have that peace even in times of upheaval. To reach that goal, we have to realize that peace is not the absence of chaos. Real peace keeps us despite the chaos, because Jesus *is* our peace. He has overcome all things, including the uncertainties of this life.

OUR ATTITUDE TOWARD PEACE

How we see peace has everything to do with how we experience it. Because we are human, we prefer lives without strife and trouble. But is a life of only good days sustainable or even possible in a fallen world? Can every day be perfect? And can we expect everyone in our circles (including ourselves) to stay on the right side of everyone else?

Of course not! That is why we spend billions of dollars each year on products and services that promise to salvage our peace—everything from aromatherapy to psychotherapy and prescription medications. For the record, I think all of these have their place and can be beneficial when used wisely. Where our quest gets sticky is when we believe that life is supposed to be peaceful and must be peaceful, all the time. When that is our expectation, even the slightest disruption seems like an existential threat that we must eliminate.

For example, if you see peace as being owed to you, you will probably end up resenting anyone and anything that interrupts it. From that perspective, uncertainty is your mortal enemy—not because it is, but because you believe it is. Therefore, you go beyond desiring certainty to demanding and even engineering it. Unfortunately, your demand can never be fully met. Uncertainty exists whether you like it or not. And you cannot possibly engineer a life of continuous certainty. Therefore, your expectations will end in frustration.

So what exactly is certainty? According to one definition, a certainty is something "definite; fixed ... inevitable ... established beyond doubt or question; indisputable ... capable of being relied on; dependable."[6] Conversely, uncertainty is the condition of being unsure about someone or something. When you are unsure, you lack conviction. You feel that if someone or something can't be relied upon, you won't dare trust it.

At times, your reluctance is wise. If you are in an abusive relationship, you cannot rely on your abuser to keep you safe or respect appropriate boundaries. But when your reluctance to trust or rely on others (or on God) becomes generalized, the consequences reach beyond a specific situation and can distort your view of all other situations. You can make a law out of distrusting your circumstances and key relationships. Add to that a wariness of the times in which you live, and you can become incredibly insecure and fearful. When this happens occasionally, you can call it a rough day. But if it becomes a chronic, pervading view of reality, your anger and resentment can dig a pit so deep, there seems no way to escape.

A major key to avoiding the pit is to dispel the misconception that peace and uncertainty are mutually exclusive, so that if one is present, the other must be absent. I would propose that millions of people believe this. Therefore, peace and uncertainty cannot coexist in their lives. If anything or anyone seems unreliable in any way, people with this mind-set have no choice but to resign themselves to turmoil. For them, peace is only possible when every single person and circumstance becomes entirely trustworthy and predictable—something that will never happen in this life!

Seeing peace and uncertainty as mutually exclusive conditions will lead you far astray. First of all, your sense of what is reliable is subjective. It is based on your personal experience and opinion, both of which can change. Therefore, it is virtually impossible for anyone to meet all of your expectations. And even if every human being defined perfection exactly as you do, such perfection would rarely, if ever, happen. You cannot expect or rely on people and circumstances to eliminate the uncertainty in your life. To expect that is to invite disappointment and disillusionment.

Uncertainty and Faith

If you really want peace, you might as well admit that uncertainty is here to stay. Believers aren't exempt, either. If you marvel at the story of Abraham, you know that uncertainty is an essential element in the life of faith. When Abraham embarked on his journey with God, uncertainty was inherent to his experience. Scripture says, "It was by faith that Abraham obeyed when God called him to leave home and go to another land that God would give him as his inheritance. *He went without knowing where he was going*" (Heb. 11:8).

Can you see why Abraham is called the father of faith? He agreed to pack up and go without having a clue where he was headed. He simply got in the yoke with God and put one foot in front of the other. That is faith, and it happens only where uncertainty exists. If the outcome of a particular journey is assured before you obey God, you don't need faith and can't even use the faith you have! You can only kick back and revel in your certainty. But be aware of the downside: if you lacked faith before the journey started, you will lack faith when it ends. And because certainty is so rare, that lack will hurt you down the road. Uncertainty is absolutely inescapable. Your faith will not eliminate it, but faith will keep it from paralyzing you.

We can learn from Abraham's faith, but our primary example is Jesus, "the champion who initiates and perfects our faith" (Heb. 12:2). He is our champion, but not because He eliminated uncertainty. Notice what Jesus said when a hopeful future follower approached him:

> *Someone came up to Jesus and said, "I want to follow you wherever you go." Jesus replied, "Yes, but remember this: even animals in the field have holes in the ground to sleep in, and birds have their nests, but the Son of Man has no place to lay down his head"* (Luke 9:57–58 TPT).

Four verses earlier, the people of a certain village had turned Jesus away. His disciples were so angered that they said, "Lord, if you wanted to, you could command fire to fall down from heaven, just as Elijah did and destroy all these wicked people" (Luke 9:54 TPT). In other words, "You could have used Your power to control those people and eliminate any uncertainty about Your visit. You could have showed them who is boss!"

When Jesus talked about having no place to lay His head, He showed His disciples that control and certainty were not His objectives. He accepted uncertainty and modeled a willingness to deal with it. Jesus Christ, the Son of God, did not see certainty as His right! Nor did He seek to control people and situations for His own benefit. When that village rejected Him, He simply went on to another one. He adjusted to their blunder and changed His plans. He did not lose His peace, and He did not use *control* to keep it.

> *The temptations in your life are no different from what others experience. And God is faithful. He will not allow the temptation to be more than you can stand. When you are tempted, he will show you a way out so that you can endure (1 Corinthians 10:13).*

The Real Issue Is Control

Jesus' response to uncertainty is exactly the opposite of what we tend to do. In order to preserve our sense of peace, we attack the uncertainty that we see as a threat. The only human means by which we can attempt this is control. That means engineering the situation so that nothing and no one has the power to make us unsure of the outcome. In other words, we become control freaks! It is a knee-jerk, fear-based, human reaction to the absolute certainty of uncertainty. Really, it's a form of denial. We convince ourselves that control can preserve our peace of mind, when nothing could be further from the truth. Trying to control everything can never succeed, except in draining the control freak's physical and emotional energy.

Where control is concerned, there is always irony. We don't realize that our attempts to control uncertainty expose the very thing that is controlling us—the fear of uncertainty! What a vicious cycle it is, and it is entirely based on a lie! Uncertainty does not result from our failure to control everything. Uncertainty is present no matter how much control we exert. Control will never ensure the certainty of our relationships and outcomes. We want to believe that it will, because we want to eliminate our anxiety. When we think our mission is accomplished, we assume that there is nothing left to fear. What we think is peace then returns, but not for long.

Are you seeing the absurdity of such thinking? It is a house of cards—a false hope in the extreme. The older I get, the more I realize how little I can control in this world. Almost every situation I face involves other people, and I have little or no control over them. I was not created to control them in the first place! Nor were they created to be controlled. Anything I can achieve through pressure will be temporary and will cause more harm than good.

Have you seen this happen in your life? Do you see how futile it is? People don't always see or do things the way you see or do them. How could they? They aren't you. They are also dealing with their own need or desire for control. They are trying to ensure certainty in their lives, and that might put them at odds with the certainty you seek. You can try to bend them to your will, but you probably have your hands full trying to bend your own will. The only control you have (if you have any at all) is over *your* thoughts, actions, and beliefs.

There is another very serious problem with the idea of control: it is an unholy trait inherited at the fall in the garden of Eden. It comes from Satan, who desires to control everything. Instead of producing certainty, control creates future problems and alienates us from those around us, including those we love most. No one wants to live with, work with, or play with a control freak. When we try controlling friends and loved ones in order to keep them close, we only increase our uncertainty and drive away the people we hold dear.

Control damages everyone and everything it touches. Although control freaks work hard to keep people in their orbit, they also tend to eject those who refuse to be controlled. At least in part, they blame these "uncontrollable" people for the uncertainty that is driving their own fear. At some point, the only people left are those who are too weary to walk away.

Control is a strong barrier to peace. It amplifies anguish and forfeits what Jesus offers, including His peace (John 14:27, 16:33). The only path to peace is kingdom living through Christ. Your peace is not dependent upon keeping people and situations in check. Your peace comes from experiencing Christ!

PEACE FROM THE PRINCE OF PEACE

What the world calls *peace* is not the peace that Jesus offers. He told His disciples, "I leave the gift of peace with you—my peace. Not the kind of fragile peace given by the world, but my perfect peace. Don't yield to fear or be troubled in your hearts—instead, be courageous!" (John 14:27 TPT). That single verse is packed with insight into the peace that Jesus gives, so let's take His statements one at a time:

- Jesus described His peace as His gift to us. That means we cannot earn it or find it anywhere else. Only He can give us His peace.

- He said that His peace is not fragile or breakable. It is not like the world's peace, which shatters easily and often. His peace is sturdy.

- He also said that His peace is perfect. No form of peace can surpass His piece or claim to be perfect.

- He told His disciples not to yield to fear but to be courageous. That tells us that conflict and uncertainty do not threaten His peace. When fear cannot dominate, peace thrives. But when peace is supplanted by fear, fear and its companions—anxiety, worry, and stress—will find their place.

That last point is less about Jesus' peace and more about us. Jesus is our peace and the giver of peace. But we have a part to play: we are not to be afraid. When we refuse to give fear the place it seeks, His gift of peace keeps us. Jesus said, "That's my parting gift to you. Peace. I don't leave you the way you're used to being left—feeling abandoned, bereft. So don't be upset. Don't be distraught" (John 14:27 MSG).

What a promise this is! But what comes first—His peace or our decision to reject fear? I think most people would love for His peace to come first and ward off all anxiety and uncertainty. But if you examine that idea closely, you find just another attempt at control, this time by involving Jesus. We want "peace insurance" in advance, so we can rest easy. We say, "Give me the insurance, and then I'll have peace." But God's kingdom does not work through guarantees. It works by faith. First, we reject fear by faith. *Then* His peace reigns and empowers us.

Your part is to reject fear at the outset, which is simpler than you think: you simply exchange something greater for something lesser. God's promises are greater (in scope, power, and importance) than the uncertainty you face, which is lesser by comparison. Your uncertainty comes from not knowing ahead of time how a particular situation will turn out. But you can know some things in advance. You know that Jesus is fully aware of your future and everything you will face. You know that He promised never to leave you (Heb. 13:5). You also know that God will work through your circumstances for your good (Rom. 8:28). His promises are greater than your uncertainty because He does not change and cannot lie (Heb. 6:18). Therefore, you can drive your stake into the ground with confidence and refuse to bow to the lesser uncertainty of whatever problems are confronting you. In the light of the Almighty, they are *nothing*!

When you remain focused on what you know about God, the gift of peace that Jesus gave you actively strengthens and encourages you. But be patient! Most situations do not resolve instantaneously. Wait courageously and pray! Paul wrote, "Don't worry over anything whatever; tell God every detail of your needs in earnest and thankful prayer, and the peace of God which transcends human understanding, will keep constant guard over your hearts and minds as they rest in Christ Jesus" (Phil. 4:6–7 PHILLIPS).

Paul's instruction, by the Spirit, is so simple that anyone can follow it! Don't worry *at all*. Refuse to fret. When fear tries to capture your heart, slam the door and say, "No!" Then go ahead and pray to your heavenly Father about the matter, giving Him thanks as you do. That is how perfect peace fixes your heart and mind on Jesus!

Anyone *can* do what Paul instructed. The Holy Spirit does not ask us to do what cannot be done. But will we obey? In the end, what matters is what we believe or don't believe and what we are willing or unwilling to act upon. So do you believe the enemy when he accuses God of not caring? Or do you believe that God is aware of your every concern? Do you believe that you are headed for doom? Or do you believe that your heavenly Father is working for your good? Are you willing to exercise self-discipline and self-control by refusing to surrender to anxiety and worry? Or will you let fear and its minions control you? Do you believe that you must control the circumstances surrounding you? Or do you believe that God's outcome is best, even when it looks different from what you have in mind?

Asking yourself questions and answering them honestly will help you to discover what makes you tick. Don't be afraid to tell yourself the truth. You will learn from what you say!

See Uncertainty as an Opportunity

When uncertainty rattles your cage, the easiest response is to surrender to fear. In the long term, however, you will regret it. So why not beat fear at its own game? You can do it by seeing uncertainty in a different light—not as an enemy but an opportunity. Let the uncertainty you hate test what you believe and trust.

Your opportunity might not come in the form of brain surgery. It might come dressed as a financial crisis or a difficult situation involving a child or other loved one who is struggling. Whatever the challenge, let it serve you. Use it to search your heart, try your faith, and expose your belief systems. If you are willing, you can experience growth. Then, when adversity comes calling again, you will be better able to cope and less prone to despair.

Remember to exchange your lesser uncertainty for the greater certainty of God's promises. That is what I do when my loss of sight makes my footing unsure. I treat my next step as another opportunity to trust in the greater One who is more real and trustworthy than the uncertainty ahead of me. As I do this, I become more aware of how He is leading me. This opens my spiritual eyes to what my natural eyes cannot see. Each step becomes an opportunity to adjust, and each step makes me more confident of the way forward.

The peace of God truly surpasses our understanding (Phil. 4:7). In that peace, we find all that we need to take the next step and meet the future with joy and the expectation of good. We are not alone. *Ever.*

LIVE AND LEARN

- In the past, how have you tended to define *peace*, and under what circumstances have you found yourself at peace? Based on what you have read in this chapter, what adjustments might help where your view of peace is concerned?

- Apart from preferring its opposite, describe your relationship with uncertainty. How does it make you feel, and how do you typically respond to it? What makes you more uncomfortable: memories of past experiences with uncertainty or a fear of unknown future outcomes? Why?

- How does the discussion of control affect your ideas about peace and uncertainty? Is it possible that your desire for a good outcome causes you to unwittingly control others? Have you ever feared that a lack of control was the cause of your adversity? In retrospect, how was your assessment accurate or inaccurate?

PART III

Making Room for Victory

10

DEFEATING SHAME, REJECTION, AND POWERLESSNESS

——◆·◆——

The Lord Yahweh empowers me, so I am not humili-
ated. For that reason, with holy determination, I will
do his will and not be ashamed.

—*Isaiah 50:7 TPT*

H as a vague, uneasy feeling ever taken root in your life
and refused to leave? I had one right after doctors recommended my brain surgery. I knew the feeling was there, but
I couldn't quite identify it. If I had felt fearful or nervous, I
would have understood. Everything I held dear was about to
be tested, and brain surgery isn't something you do every day.
But for all the reasons I described earlier, fear was not the issue.
There was something else, a kind of emotional undertow that
kept tugging at me. I knew that it involved my diagnosis, but I
did not know how.

Then one day, it dawned on me: I was ashamed! I'll tell you
why in a moment, but first, let's take a look at shame itself.

The Start of Shame

If you know the story of Adam and Eve, you know that they walked Planet Earth in their birthday suits—not as adorable, dimpled babies but as full-grown adults. They never considered a dress code, because they were not ashamed or embarrassed by their uncovered state. Shame and embarrassment would not have occurred to them, because complete innocence was all they knew. They had done nothing wrong and had been created naked by God. From their untainted frame of reference, they never saw themselves as being naked at all.

The serpent made sure that their blessed blamelessness did not last. When Adam and Eve ate the fruit that God forbade them to eat, their perspective changed instantly. Here is how the Bible describes the transformation:

> *At that moment their eyes were opened, and they suddenly felt shame at their nakedness. So they sewed fig leaves together to cover themselves. When the cool evening breezes were blowing, the man and his wife heard the LORD God walking about in the garden. So they hid from the LORD God among the trees. Then the LORD God called to the man, "Where are you?" He replied, "I heard you walking in the garden, so I hid. I was afraid because I was naked" (Genesis 3:7–10).*

Shame devastates the human soul and fractures our ability to relate to others. Adam and Eve were accustomed to being with God in the garden. The fellowship they shared with Him and with one another was seamless and uninhibited, because they had no fear and nothing to hide. But when sin rearranged their perspectives, their thoughts and ways of seeing God and others became rooted in fear. God knew that but wanted to help them to understand what sin had accomplished. So He asked them a profound question: "*Who told you* that you were naked? … Have you eaten from the tree whose fruit I commanded you not to eat?" (Gen. 3:11).

Shame originated on that day, in that garden. Sin erected a barrier between Adam and Eve and God. It introduced thoughts and emotions that Adam and Eve had never experienced. Up to that point, nakedness, fear, and shame were nonissues. The serpent knew that and accused God of withholding knowledge from Adam and Eve. When they accepted the serpent's offer, everything changed. All that was pure became tainted. Innocence turned to shame. Acceptance suddenly seemed conditional, and trouble plagued humanity.

Imagine the impact of sin's entrance on the psyches of God's first man and woman. No longer carefree in God's love, they turned inward and covered up, both literally and figuratively. Instead of continuing in blissful and open communion with God, they hid from Him. Instead of being blameless, they felt exposed, disgraced, and afraid.

IDENTIFYING SHAME

Having a clear picture of shame makes it easier to detect its operation. Shame can be described as "a painful emotion caused by a strong sense of guilt, embarrassment, unworthiness, or disgrace."[7] It is "the painful sense that you lack value as a person … are defective, worthless, unlovable. It is not simply that something is wrong with your behavior, it is that something is wrong with *you as a person.*"[8]

In one way or another, everyone experiences shame. Because it is so painful, we often bury our shame under masks and layers of performance. Although shame can cause feelings of guilt, it is not the same as guilt. Guilt is a fact related to our sense of responsibility for certain actions or failures to act. We feel guilty when we hurt our loved ones with harsh words or keep secrets from them. Shame is different; it comes from the deep belief that we are inherently defective. When we believe that, we get stuck, because we cannot separate ourselves from our defects. Our shame follows us wherever we go, regardless of what we accomplish in life. Until we uncover the shame and recognize the lie that produces it, shame will continue nagging and lying to us.

That explains my sense of shame over having a brain tumor. I was not *guilty* of having a brain tumor. But at the root of my strange unease was the idea that I was defective. It would be a matter of time before I would be tempted to hide my defect or mask it in some way.

Can you relate to what I am saying? Have you ever reached for a fig leaf to cover up what makes you ashamed? Whether you do it consciously or not, you are attempting to hide your defect and avoid rejection, from people and from God. Because you feel unworthy, you separate yourself from God and stop taking your needs to Him. You can stop praying altogether, even when you desperately need Him!

You can see how damaging shame is. It strangles your relationships and makes you more vulnerable to Satan—which, from his perspective, is the perfect setup. This is why it is so important to uncover shame. Once you identify it, you can dismantle it! When I identified what made me feel ashamed, I had to figure out why I saw it as a defect. In time, I realized that a wrong perspective of my Christian testimony was in play. Somehow, I felt that I had "allowed" my tumor to happen. In allowing it, I had failed God and His people.

Thankfully, the Holy Spirit shone His light on the shame and everything that was feeding it. He took me back to things I already knew but had lost sight of where my illness was concerned. He reminded me that my worth and value were not determined by the condition of my brain or any other part of my being. Therefore, having a tumor did not make me a defective Christian. Because I accepted Jesus Christ as my Lord and Savior, God declared me worthy of eternal life and adoption into His family. It had nothing to do with who I was or what I had done. He did not deem me worthy because I was a "good" person. He deemed me worthy because He cleansed my unworthy spirit. I was already valuable because He created me. Then He ransomed me back from sin at the highest possible cost: the life of Jesus. It did not make me a perfect human being, but it delivered me from shame. And it continues to remind me that I am worthy in God's eyes.

Friend, if your life is hidden with Christ in God and you are going through affliction or any other type of adversity, you are not defective! Receive God's love and encouragement and reject the shame that works to isolate you. Let God's own Word wash over you and refute any sense of shame that tries to attach itself to your life. This passage from Romans is a great place to start:

> Having been justified by faith, we have peace with God through our Lord Jesus Christ, through whom also we have access by faith into this grace in which we stand, and rejoice in hope of the glory of God. And not only that, but we also glory in tribulations, knowing that tribulation produces perseverance; and perseverance, character; and character, hope. Now hope does not disappoint, because the love of God has been poured out in our hearts by the Holy Spirit who was given to us (Romans 5:1–5 NKJV).

You might experience suffering in your adversity, but there is no shame in that, because the love of God has settled your worth. Paul wrote to his protégé, Timothy, about this very thing. Take a good look at what he said:

The confidence of my calling enables me to overcome every difficulty without shame, for I have an intimate revelation of this God. And my faith in him convinces me that he is more than able to keep all that I've placed in his hands safe and secure until the fullness of his appearing (2 Timothy 1:12 TPT).

Paul overcame difficulty and avoided shame because he had an "intimate revelation" of God. Shame will knock on your door, but you don't have to invite it in and serve it tea. Shame is part of the fallen nature. Your answer to the fallen nature is your redemption and the new mentality it creates! If Christ is your Lord and Savior, your mistakes and shortcomings do not determine your worth and value. So stop measuring yourself against a false standard that says you come up short. Stop shaming yourself!

I prayed to the LORD, and he answered me. He freed me from all my fears. Those who look to him for help will be radiant with joy; no shadow of shame will darken their faces (Psalms 34:4–5).

You Are Valid

We humans are born needing validation, not because we were created invalid but because we were born into sin. To *validate* is "to recognize, establish, or illustrate the worthiness or legitimacy of" someone or something."[9] When we are growing up, validation from our parents and other caregivers helps us to develop a healthy self-image and sense of self-worth that make us less likely to crave validation as adults.

When you feel validated, you accept your legitimacy as a human being. You know that you are an authentic creation of the living God and not an imposter. You can feel comfortable in your own skin and unthreatened by other people's positive attributes. If this issue is not settled in your heart, you will be more apt to bend to other people's expectations in order to prove your legitimacy and receive validation. But the harder you work to receive it, the less legitimate you feel.

The ultimate source of your validation is the One who created you. The finished work of the cross makes you wholly acceptable to God. Knowing this makes you far less vulnerable to external pressures. Extended periods of adversity can still cause you to misunderstand your struggles, however. When you think that God is not intervening on your behalf, you can wonder whether you are worthy of His involvement. Then you can start trying to prove your worth all over again.

Recognize the trap and resist it! You are not called to prove yourself. You have been validated by God, not for your performance or because you are a perfect specimen (there is no such thing), but because you have accepted the sacrifice of the Lamb and are God's child. Children are worthy of their Father's love, and your heavenly Father gives His love freely. Through the new birth, your validation is assured. Your worth and legitimacy are embedded in your salvation. The issue was settled at the cross, and the enemy of your soul knows it!

THE FEAR OF REJECTION

Before Adam and Eve sinned, they felt fully accepted and loved by God and each other. But after they sinned, their assurance was replaced with another new fear: the fear of rejection. This fear touches every human being and has the potential to taint every relationship. You can fear being rejected by friends, loved ones, schoolmates, or even the dominant culture (the church of Jesus Christ is susceptible to this one). This fear promotes people-pleasing and a performance mentality designed to win over those whose rejection you fear, including a perfectionist parent, a controlling boss, or your spouse. It is a flawed strategy, because you will never perform perfectly or please everyone. Yet your fear of rejection will pressure you to try.

If you are a Christian, the fear of rejection can rear its head when you share your faith with friends and acquaintances. Terrified of causing anyone to reject Christ or His body, you try to present the gospel in the least "offensive" way possible, even to the point of diluting it. The truth is that some people will reject the message regardless of your efforts. Some might even reject you for sharing it. That is their choice. Just remember that they are not really rejecting you. They are rejecting Christ.

Like adversity and uncertainty, rejection is a fact of life. Some people reject those whom they see as being "less than" themselves. Others use rejection preemptively when they feel "less than" the people they reject. The point is that you cannot control people's choices, and their rejection has no bearing on your worth. Even Jesus, the only perfect man to walk the earth "was despised and rejected" by others (Isa. 53:3).

The important thing is how you respond to rejection. Will you take it personally and devalue yourself because of it? Or will you let it roll off your back and move on? Either way, your response reflects your sense of identity (which we will discuss in the next chapter). When your identity is solid and you know that your worth and value do not change according to other people's opinions, their rejection will not set you back.

And it shouldn't! Just prepare your heart with the truth, because rejection is bound to come. Become consciously aware of how it has triggered you in the past. Bring that before God and let Him remind you of who you are in His eyes. Do this consistently and the fear of rejection (which can be uglier than the rejection itself) will not control you.

FEELINGS OF POWERLESSNESS

When I awakened from my first forty-eight hours in the hospital, I was shocked to hear all that happened while I was asleep. When I tried to express my astonishment, I realized that I could not speak and I realized that I could not see out of my right eye. The first problem was temporary; I could not speak because of my breathing tube. But the vision problem was a blow, especially when I learned that doctors considered it to be permanent.

I felt utterly powerless. It was not a vague or hidden feeling. It was front and center, and I recognized it immediately. But powerlessness isn't always experienced that way. Sometimes the feeling hovers just below the level of your consciousness and gnaws at you from the shadows. Either way, it takes a toll, so it is important to be detect it. We need to identify when and why we feel powerless. Then we can consciously and accurately evaluate our reactions and subject them to God's truth.

If you suspect that a sense of powerlessness could be flying under your radar, look for telltale signs in your words and thoughts. Perhaps the following sound familiar:

"I can't take much more of this! How long is this going to continue?"

"My life is totally out of control."

"I can't live like this!"

These are expressions of powerlessness, and all of us have heard them in our hearts. Sometimes, unwelcome surprises come out of nowhere and clip us behind the knees. The greater the impact, the more powerless we feel. Often, instead of acknowledging these feelings and putting them in perspective, we wrestle with them and give them more of our mental and emotional energy. The real issue, I believe, involves our expectations where powerlessness is concerned. If we consciously examine our expectations, our feelings of powerlessness can dissipate rather than intensify.

For example, do you feel that Christians should never feel powerless? If so, your expectation can set you up for a double whammy. Not only will you have to confront your feelings of powerlessness, but you will also have to deal with the inner conflict your misplaced expectation created. I say "misplaced" because Christians can feel powerlessness in certain situations. There are times when not feeling powerless would be absurd! Can you imagine watching the Twin Towers crumble on 9/11 without feeling powerless to stop them?

The important thing is what you believe about your feelings of powerlessness and how you process them. They may come, but they do not have to take over. God is there, and His power will carry you through your storm. Lean into Him, and you will come to grips with the situation. When you approach feelings of powerlessness this way, they cannot own you. You know that you are not going to be destroyed. With God's help, you will take one step at a time, and He will lead you to the other side of your difficulty.

Processing your feelings of powerlessness is so important! If you let them process you, they can become chronic, leading to depression, frustration, oppression, and feelings of deprivation. Don't dismiss your sense of powerlessness or try to reason your way out of it. And don't sweep it under the rug. Denying how you feel will only leave you feeling less empowered and more prone to fear and anger. Then you might find yourself accusing God of not caring enough to intervene and deliver you.

That is a tipping point you do not want to reach. What you need in your anger is exactly opposite to what your anger demands. You need God! You need to yoke yourself with Jesus and draw from Him the strength and comfort you need and want. Becoming adversarial and alienated from Him only distances you from the source of your hope. The devil would love nothing more than to lead you around by your anger. Don't give him the opportunity. His suggestions will only deepen your frustration and drive you to a place where no victory or joy can be found.

Understanding and self-awareness are keys to recognizing how powerlessness is triggered and how you can put it in check. One of the most obvious causes of feeling powerless is realizing that you cannot produce the changes you desire. For example, if loved ones insist on making poor choices, you can feel powerless to help them. You know you cannot force them to change. And, depending upon their frame of mind, they might even refuse your help. Another cause of feeling powerless is the realization that you don't control the duration of a particular crisis. This is true of layoffs, pandemics, and monster storms, for example. The scale of these events can trigger a sense of powerlessness for large numbers of people and even entire populations!

So how can we respond to our feelings of powerlessness in productive ways? First and foremost, we can put our hope in God's truth, which sets us free (John 8:32). Because we live in a fallen world, we can expect to encounter forces of evil. Evil is nothing new, and as much as it grieves us, it is not our biggest problem. If it were, we would have no choice but to believe we are destined to live in unceasing pain and distress. After all, if we cannot prevent pandemics or hurricanes, we certainly cannot banish evil from the earth.

Our biggest problems are the unscriptural things we believe about life. Do we believe that our hard work and right choices should earn us the good life? Do we believe that right living is an insurance policy against the world's evil, injustice, and selfishness? Beliefs like these set us up for untruthful perspectives that leave us ill-equipped for adversity. If our beliefs are distorted by misunderstandings of Scripture or teachings that selectively draw on Scripture, we cannot help but feel powerless and even betrayed when reality proves our assumptions wrong.

To free ourselves, we need to reject our mistaken beliefs and relentlessly pursue the truth. We need to get real where our faith is concerned and not sell ourselves on falsehoods that tickle our ears. Tribulation is not a fluke or aberration; it is exactly what Jesus told us to expect. He said in no uncertain terms that it would come to all of us (John 16:33). Instead of getting angry about it, let's seek Him until we find the strength, courage, and grace to meet and emerge from every challenge. Instead of being powerless, let's be empowered by the Spirit of God to see as He sees and respond as He would have us respond. We can trust Him. He is faithful!

LIVE AND LEARN

- How has the lie that something is wrong—not just with what you do, but with whom you are—affected your day-to-day life? How might our discussion of shame shed light on certain painful experiences from the past and/or redefine them?

- Think about your most memorable experiences with rejection. How did they make you feel? How might you respond differently to similar situations today? Why would you respond differently, and how does that help you put your past rejection experiences into perspective?

- When have you felt most powerless? Was the feeling short-lived, or did it linger (and if so, what was the cost)? How might you adjust your perspective regarding powerlessness in a current situation? Are you as powerless as you think you are? Explain.

11

IDENTITY IN ADVERSITY

———◆———

*Once you were full of darkness, but now you have light
from the Lord. So live as people of light! For this light
within you produces only what is good and right and
true. —Ephesians 5:8–9*

In the crush of adversity, feelings of shame, illegitimacy, rejection, and powerlessness can surface, turning our seasons of adversity into seasons of soul-searching. It is natural to look inward when our assumptions seem not to be working. It is also an important part of becoming more self-aware. But unless we bare our souls before God and let Him guide our discovery, the inward search can turn to the kind of navel-gazing that only increases turmoil and confusion.

I found my share of navel-gazing opportunities after I learned about the tumor in my brain. The diagnosis and its aftermath came with feelings of shame and powerlessness that forced me to seek God and His truth. He showed me that the tumor did not make me a defective Christian, and He helped me to balance my sense of powerlessness with the realities of His Word. He gave me the clarity I needed to cooperate more fully with my recovery and His view of my calling.

My feelings of shame and powerlessness were not random. They happened in the larger context of my identity. Whether consciously or not, I did what we humans tend to do: I tied my trauma to unspoken views about who I was. I inspected my identity for flaws that allowed a tumor to invade in my brain, and I wondered how I might have invited the incursion. When I took these concerns to the Lord, He answered with a simple question: "Are your wrongs forgiven, or aren't they?"

Only one answer was possible: "Yes, Lord! They are."

That was huge, but there was more work to do. I still wondered whether my illness disqualified me for ministry. I felt that I'd let down the people I serve by not embodying the faith that I preach. Something buried in my belief systems told me that I needed to be strong, otherwise I could not help them—as though *my* strength were what they needed! The real issue had little to do with my strength and everything to do with my affliction. A lie was at work—the lie that attributes all affliction to sin.

The irony is that I never consciously believed any such thing. I did not blame people's illnesses on their sin and did not see their medical issues as spiritual "scarlet letters." I never preached that and never discredited other leaders who got sick. Yet when I got sick, adversity opened a doorway of attack and exposed a lie that I applied to myself. This vulnerability became even more apparent when doctors declared my partial loss of sight to be medically permanent. I felt a barrage arrayed against me, both physically and in terms of my identity!

Adversity challenged me, awakened me to a preexisting vulnerability, and invited me to purge my misconception. Until I did, my adversity would define me and become my taskmaster. I knew there could be no victory in that! Adversity would give way to victory only if I consciously defined my trial *and my identity* in terms of my life in Christ.

YOUR INHERENT VALUE AND YOUR ADVERSITY

Let me say yet again that as God's creation, you are inherently valuable. Period. Full stop. Whether you feel confident of that fact or not, it is true. Your worth is nonnegotiable. When you see yourself this way, you tend to have a positive self-image, which means you feel good about yourself. This is relevant to adversity because a positive self-image increases your sense of stability. When you value yourself, you know that you have something to offer. You are more open to opportunity and more likely to help yourself and others. You understand that you are not here by accident, and you acknowledge your reason for being. You see your seasons of adversity within a larger context, and you do not define yourself according to your troubles.

Those who question their worth tend to experience life very differently. If you are among them, you might struggle with anxiety and emotional lows that degrade your confidence and sap your emotional strength. When trials place greater demands on your mind and body, your anxiety can become chronic, making your emotional lows even harder to handle. Instead of feeling good about yourself and developing a sense of stability, you feel vulnerable. In your heightened emotional state, you can misinterpret God's intent and interpret His silence as a rejection of your validity, as though you and your situation are not worthy of His involvement.

Whether your self-image is positive or negative, you are evaluating yourself and your worth. We all do this, often without realizing it. I believe that we do it because we know instinctively that God has placed in us great value and purpose. During our adversity, however, our self-assessments can become distorted. Upheaval can trick us into seeing the changes that have occurred—the losses, the sicknesses, the financial setbacks, and the relational struggles—as deductions from our value as human beings. Making this calculation can devastate us, but it

127

is bad math! We are subtracting points from the wrong column! Our value as people does not change because of external events or our handling of those events. Our value as people is fixed by God. So when we devalue ourselves during the hard times, our adversity is not the real issue. It simply reveals a misunderstanding of our identity and worth.

Identity and the New Creation

Your sense of personal worth stems from your identity and shapes your self-image. If you are in Christ, any sense of unworthiness defies the truth of who you are in Him. If He is your Lord and Savior, you are a new creation. The apostle Paul understood this, and it governed how he saw other people. Look at what he said:

> So from now on we don't think of anyone from a human point of view. If we did think of Christ from a human point of view, we don't anymore. Whoever is a believer in Christ is a new creation. The old way of living has disappeared. A new way of living has come into existence (2 Corinthians 5:16–17 GW).

We need these words to become flesh in us! Otherwise, we can claim they are true yet deny them in practice. How? By professing that we are His yet living as though we were orphans. Are we new creatures, or aren't we? If we are, we ought to live the way new creatures live!

The passage from Second Corinthians shows that transformation was Paul's way of life. The love of Christ so changed him that He saw people in a new way. Remember that he once hunted down Jesus' followers, and he did it proudly. But being a new creation revolutionized his point of view. He became acutely aware that our value, and other people's value, comes from the God who created us and the Savior who paid the price of our redemption.

Revisiting these truths will help you get free, and they will keep you free! Neither you nor any person or situation can alter your worth and value. They are not changed by what you do or don't do. They weren't based on your actions in the first place! If you are in Christ, your identity in Him determines your worth, and the "certificate" of your worth is contained in the vault of your born-again spirit.

You saw me before I was born. Every day of my life was recorded in your book. Every moment was laid out before a single day had passed. How precious are your thoughts about me, O God. They cannot be numbered! I can't even count them; they outnumber the grains of sand! And when I wake up, you are still with me! (Psalms 139:16–18)

YOUR IDENTITY HISTORY

Confusion and inner conflicts over identity usually originate in childhood. If you were raised to feel loved, valued, and cherished, you are likely to see yourself as being lovable, valuable, and worthy. This makes it easier for you to engage with others, love them, and assume that they value you. If, on the other hand, you were tolerated rather than cherished and went mostly ignored or unnoticed, you will tend to see yourself as being unimportant, uninteresting, and unworthy of other people's attention. You will tend to be aloof, tentative, and relationally unavailable, because you believe that you are not valued by others.

Do you see how the past shapes your sense of identity and even your behaviors? If you identify as someone who has been hurt, dumped on, or abused, you will likely gravitate to relationships that make you feel the same way—not because those feelings are pleasant, but because they are familiar, and you identify with them. Their gravitational pull can become so habit-forming that you subconsciously orchestrate similar situations, believing that you are skilled in navigating them.

What you learn at a young age often "prophesies" to your future. If your sense of worth and value in childhood came from other people's reactions to your conduct, you will tend to draw your identity from your performance in adulthood. The standard of measure that others applied in the past becomes the measure you apply to yourself now. If the standard from childhood was unattainable—if your grades were never high enough, your aspirations were never important enough, or your efforts were never satisfactory—you will hold yourself to an equally unreachable standard as an adult. This unforgiving measuring stick will reinforce your inadequacy and diminish your sense of well-being, causing bitterness, anger, dissatisfaction, and malaise to flourish.

The sense of worth and value first formed in childhood transfers to your adulthood, along with your reliance on other people's input in forming your self-image. Whether they are your friends, coworkers, or your spouse, you will place yourself at their mercy. Unless their emotional and verbal feedback are consistently positive, you will be hard-pressed to feel good about yourself. And until you can feel good about yourself, stability will be hard to find.

IDENTITY IN ALL THE WRONG PLACES

Performance-based patterns from our youth train us to seek our identity in all the wrong places. Whether because of upbringing or culture, millions or even billions of people find their identity and worth in their work or station in life. From that perspective, real-life rocket scientists might evaluate themselves based on the world's view that they are intelligent and highly skilled. Some might even derive their sense of security from their standing in the aerospace community.

But what happens when rocket scientists become unable to function in their expert capacities? How do they feel when age or sudden impairments end their scientific careers? Are these accomplished people doomed to feeling "less than"?

For some rocket scientists and many other people, the answer would be *yes*. Unless you believe that your identity is settled in Christ, your sense of self will fluctuate based on your sense of usefulness, your moods and emotions, your most recent "performances," and the opinions of others—some of the most unreliable indicators imaginable! And none of them legitimately determine who you are.

Another illegitimate source of identity is the surrounding culture. Currently, the culture confuses matters of identity by applying standards that its icons popularize. Whether they are politicians, performing artists, experts in various fields, or media giants, they are not qualified arbiters of authentic identity. And the standards they model often misrepresent what is admirable, promoting instead beliefs and behaviors that defy biblical mandates. Nevertheless, millions of people emulate the famous and crave their approval.

If you seek approval by meeting the standards of celebrities and their followers, you will chase a moving target all the way to your grave. Your efforts will degrade your sense of self-worth, lower your self-confidence, and reinforce a negative outlook. Instead of developing a sense of well-being, you will invite anxiety and insecurity. And instead of becoming free, you will be enslaved to the approval you crave.

What you are really looking for is not found in the ways of the world. It is found in the ways of Christ, who is never fickle but always trustworthy. Paul explained it this way:

Here's what I want you to do, God helping you: Take your everyday, ordinary life—your sleeping, eating, going-to-work, and walking-around life—and place it before God as an offering. Embracing what God does for you is the best thing you can do for him. Don't become so well-adjusted to your culture that you fit into it without even thinking. Instead, fix your attention on God. You'll be changed from the inside out. Readily recognize what he wants from you, and quickly respond to it. Unlike the culture around you, always dragging you down to its level of immaturity, God brings the best out of you, develops well-formed maturity in you (Romans 12:2 MSG).

Any soulish means of establishing identity or improving your sense of well-being will only make emotional stability harder to come by. The world is corrupted by sin. It is not geared to affirm you; its taint can only diminish, confuse, stereotype, and control you. But it can only do that with your permission.

IDENTITY IN THE ROCK

The well-being and stability you desire are found only in Christ. When you identify with Him and are in Him, you are approved, affirmed, and accepted by the only One qualified to assess your value! With your identity secured in Him, moving targets and changing circumstances cannot determine or diminish your worth and value. They will not be tied to people's opinions of you or your situation. They will be tied to the Rock Himself.

Remember: no matter how chaotic your life seems to be, God's love and validation are constant. He is not measuring you by your circumstances or by the standards others have set for you. No matter how long your adversity lasts, God's validation and approval remain. Your troubles are not evidence that you are defective. Your troubles are part of life, and they are "no different from what others experience" (1 Cor. 10:13).

Christ is the source of your identity, regardless of what the world offers or claims. As long as you are His, your righteousness is an established fact, and God's acceptance of you is unshakeable. He values you because He created you and loves you. He is not measuring you against any other human being or by any human standard. If you have measured yourself that way, it is time to stop and repent! Quit devaluing what God prizes—*you*!

LIVE AND LEARN

- Have you searched yourself for some "defect" that is responsible for your adversity? Why was your search destined to fail? What "rabbit trails" did it lead you on, and what has been the cost? Are/were you ready and willing to drop your search, and why?

- Has any recent (or other) tumultuous experience affected your sense of identity? What are some of the faulty sources from which you have attempted to draw your identity? In what ways have you successfully cherished and protected your identity in Christ?

- Which childhood experiences or patterns most shaped your sense of identity? How have they impacted your struggles in adulthood? Which ideas from this chapter are most helpful in informing a new perspective, and why?

12

GET UNSTUCK!

—◆—

I called out your name, O God, called from the bottom of the pit. You listened when I called out, "Don't shut your ears! Get me out of here! Save me!" You came close when I called out. You said, "It's going to be all right." —Lamentations 3:55–57 MSG

"Lord, I repent of self-pity." That is a one-line journal entry from my season of adversity. Like all trials, mine did not occur in a vacuum. Medical emergencies happened amid other concerns, including a painful situation that touched our family at the cellular level. When doctors told me I had a brain tumor, my heart was already breaking. My marriage was not in trouble. There was no financial devastation and no worries about the little ones we love so much. But our family, and particularly one of our daughters, experienced a season of great distress.

I remember bringing my fears and profound sense of powerlessness to the Lord. The "what-ifs" seemed overwhelming, so I ran down my list. The Lord acknowledged each item and showed me that He was already involved. He patiently helped me to process each fear, but I questioned His timeline. The family issue was causing so much pain in the short term that I could not imagine what damage the long haul might bring. I was convinced that unless breakthrough came quickly, all could be lost. There were too many ways for the situation to get worse.

After hearing me out, the Lord asked a simple question: "Would you like Me to guarantee your freedom from all anguish or destruction so that you can be at rest sooner rather than later?"

His question tweaked my focus. I knew that a microwaved solution was not what we needed and might not work in the long term. And I knew that a pain-free life was untenable. Yet the weight of the situation made me crave both. I did not have to explain, because God already knew my thoughts before I said a word (Ps. 139:4). But I needed to bare my soul to Him and examine my thoughts in His presence. So I told Him the bitter truth: "I feel like I am going through the motions of living."

My pain and disappointment were profound. I thought my whole life pointed to failure and wondered, "How could anyone witness my life and choose to follow Christ?" Shame and sadness overwhelmed me. It seemed obvious that when I thought I was giving and doing my best, I fell woefully short. I told the Lord, "I know You don't condemn me; but it gives me much more joy to bring You success than failure."

I was stuck in self-pity, insecurity, and misery! What I desperately needed was to stop focusing on myself and my cries for my child and look to God. It did not matter what I could or could not do. My ability was irrelevant. Only He could redeem the situation my family was facing. So I turned my vision to the bigger picture and the glory of God and said, "Nevertheless, You are holy. And You are the hope of my life."

Having poured out and processed my emotions and self-absorption, I repented of the self-pity that kept me in the stuck place.

Self-Pity and the Stuck Place

Self-pity, grief, and insecurity are like emotional quicksand. They don't release you just because you want out. To get free, you have to know which ditch you fell into and then learn how to climb out. One of the biggest ditches is self-pity, especially when adversity comes. The deception of self-pity is ravenous, feeding back on itself until the only thing you see is "poor me." It is also an equal-opportunity offender. You don't have to be fainthearted to feel sorry for yourself. Even stalwart prophets who risked their lives to serve God fell into self-pity.

In First Kings 18, Israel was in an extended period of drought, which Elijah had prophesied. In the drought's third year, God told Elijah to send for King Ahab and tell him that rain was coming. Ahab and his wife, Queen Jezebel, were idolators who dishonored the God of Israel, encouraged witchcraft and all types of evil, and supported hundreds of false prophets. Elijah was a thorn in their sides, and they blamed him for the drought. So when he summoned the king with good news, the king called him a "troublemaker" (1 Kings 18:17). Elijah called out the lie and helped Ahab to refresh his memory:

> "I have made no trouble for Israel," Elijah replied. "You and your family are the troublemakers, for you have refused to obey the commands of the LORD and have worshiped the images of Baal instead. Now summon all Israel to join me at Mount Carmel, along with the 450 prophets of Baal and the 400 prophets of Asherah who are supported by Jezebel." So Ahab summoned all the people of Israel and the prophets to Mount Carmel (1 Kings 18:18–20).

Elijah called for a showdown, and Ahab took him up on his offer. The false prophets would call on their god, and Elijah would call on the living God. Whoever called down fire first would declare their deity to be the true God.

Evidently, Ahab believed the fight was a fair one. However, Elijah knew better. Hundreds of false prophets were no match for the living God. From morning to evening, the wicked prophets called down fire, but nothing happened. When Elijah's turn came, he made the challenge harder: he soaked the altar, wood, and offering with water—three times. Then he called down fire. Immediately, fire came and "even licked up all the water in the trench!" (1 Kings 18:38).

Imagine what the false prophets thought about this stunning show of God's power! Afterward, Elijah had all the prophets of Baal corralled in the Kishon Valley, where he put every one of them to death. When Jezebel heard about it, she promised to kill Elijah, saying, "May the gods strike me and even kill me if by this time tomorrow I have not killed you just as you killed them" (1 Kings 19:2).

Terrified by the threat, Elijah fled. It was a stunning turn of emotions! In faith and obedience, he had participated in a great victory over the powers of darkness. Yet he was quickly reduced to a bundle of nerves. "He went on alone into the wilderness, traveling all day. He sat down under a solitary broom tree and prayed that he might die. 'I have had enough, LORD,' he said. 'Take my life, for I am no better than my ancestors who have already died'" (1 Kings 19:4).

Paralyzed by fear and dread, Elijah felt completely unable to cope. So he wrapped himself in self-pity and asked to die. He forgot that the God who just performed a massive miracle on Mount Carmel could also keep him out of Jezebel's crosshairs.

Self-pity makes us forgetful, blinds us to God's keeping power, and forms a downward spiral of hopelessness. However, not all pity is bad. When you hear about other people's hardships, you feel "sympathy and sorrow aroused by [their] misfortune or suffering."[10] That kind of pity can prompt you to comfort the hurting. But, when you pity yourself, there is no comfort. You only drill deeper into your suffering and perpetuate it. You can even become angry, believing on some level that God Himself does not expect you to endure the struggle you are in.

When you believe that you are suffering unjustly, self-pity becomes your fast friend. But it is not your friend. It is a trap! Agree with it, and it will squeeze tighter, demanding even more agreement. It will strip your motivation to break free and keep you rehearsing the unfairness of life. Self-pity can do nothing but generate more misery. Therefore, it quickly becomes your steel-reinforced stuck place!

Elijah was stuck, but Jezebel's threats were not the cause. He was trapped in his emotions. His "Woe is me!" distorted his perspective. He complained to God about how he, God's zealous prophet, had been terribly wronged. He even claimed to be the only one still serving God! So God corrected his misunderstanding and assured him that many other faithful servants "[had] never bowed down to Baal or kissed him!" (1 Kings 19:18).

When Elijah's rant was over, God instructed him, among other things, to go to Abel-meholah and anoint Elisha *to replace him as prophet* (1 Kings 19:16). Talk about a wakeup call! God gave His prophet a pink slip and sent him to install his replacement.

However, God never stopped loving or honoring Elijah. He even took him to heaven in a chariot of fire (2 Kings 2:11). Elijah stumbled, just as we stumble, but God did not walk away from him. He simply corrected him and allowed him to experience the consequences of his mistakes. From this I believe God wants us to understand how destructive self-pity is. He wants us to see how easily it embitters, blinds, and robs us of what He has in store. He wants us to realize that when we indulge in self-pity, we surrender our freedom and find it harder to receive the comfort and strength we need.

Self-pity is a thief!

Grief and the Stuck Place

Israel's beloved prophet and judge, Samuel, was another servant of God who fell into a trap—the trap of grief. While under Samuel's leadership, Israel begged to have king, like other nations had. Samuel took their demand personally and assumed that they were rejecting him. But they weren't rejecting a man; they were rejecting God.

God was not behind the Israelites' desire, yet He granted their wish and selected Saul to lead them. God shared His decision with His prophet, and Samuel anointed Saul. The new king seemed to be everything the people wanted, yet his heart was not right. Samuel instructed him in advance to destroy any spoils from Israel's war with Amalek and kill their king, Agag. But Saul chose to do things his own way. He spared Agag, saved Amalek's livestock and other choice goods, and said that he was planning to sacrifice the animals to God.

Samuel did not buy Saul's excuses. Instead, he rebuked him:

> *Samuel said, Hath the Lord as great delight in burnt offerings and sacrifices, as in obeying the voice of the Lord? Behold, to obey is better than sacrifice, and to hearken than the fat of rams. For rebellion is as the sin of witchcraft, and stubbornness is as iniquity and idolatry. Because thou hast rejected the word of the Lord, he hath also rejected thee from being king (1 Samuel 15:22–23 KJV).*

Saul insisted that he did everything God asked of him, so God stripped away his throne. This devastated Samuel. He was invested in Saul and probably believed that Saul's kingship was his fault anyway. Samuel's grief was so stubborn that God asked him, "So, how long are you going to mope over Saul? You know I've rejected him as king over Israel" (1 Sam. 16:1 MSG).

God spoke sharply to Samuel because he was stuck and struggling with the kinds of regrets that can only produce greater devastation. Samuel wondered whether he had missed God altogether, and he blamed himself for all that happened. His wallowing and self-doubt were not what Israel needed. They were in a crisis and faced losing the king they once begged God to provide. The nation desperately needed Samuel to convey God's plan and guide them through their adversity.

Most of us can relate to what Samuel felt. When life goes awry, it is easy to question what we thought was God's plan. We are quick to blame ourselves for people and things we cannot control. Although God gives us opportunities to succeed, we can fall short. Even the most promising scenarios can go sideways. It does not mean that God wasn't involved; it means that He honors our freedom to choose. He is not responsible for ensuring that everything turns out well simply because He ordained it. He calls us to partner with Him and work toward that end. When He invites us to participate, the *potential* for fulfillment is assured. But the choices we make are truly ours to make; the choices of others are not.

God did not set up Saul to fail. Saul's choices made success impossible. Samuel got stuck because he grieved over what might have been. He wanted God to fix what was broken and finish what He started with Saul. But God had already moved on. Samuel eventually followed Him, but he risked staying stuck and missing God as spectacularly as Saul had missed Him.

Insecurity and the Stuck Place

When adversity persists, uncertainty can permeate your thinking and scatter your hopes and plans. Over time, you can lapse into anxiety and a heightened sense of vulnerability.

Insecurity about your well-being and ability to handle pressure seems to appear out of nowhere. You realize that whatever made you feel secure in the past probably worked for all the wrong reasons. What you thought was "under control" really wasn't under control. Your plans and previous successes seemed to keep you safe, but you were vulnerable the whole time. And now, your adversity proves it!

We are not masters of our own fate, even when we think we are. Any security we find in ourselves and our ability is a false security birthed out of our need to feel in control. When adversity shakes what we thought was sturdy, we realize that we used emotional pacifiers to create a sense of security where there was none. The realization is unsettling because it exposes our vulnerability and drags our anxiety out into the open.

Am I suggesting that we should scrap wise planning and hard work? Absolutely not! Making life plans and working toward their fulfillment are godly pursuits. But they cannot ensure our security. Circumstances—even good circumstances—are subject to change. The unexpected can lay an axe to the root of the "perfect" plan. We need to acknowledge that and understand that we cannot build our security on anything we create. As long as we are the source of our security, we will remain unanchored and adrift.

Real security is built on the way of truth, as the Book of James explains:

> Look here, you who say, "Today or tomorrow we are going to a certain town and will stay there a year. We will do business there and make a profit." How do you know what your life will be like tomorrow? Your life is like the morning fog—it's here a little while, then it's gone. What you ought to say is, "If the Lord wants us to, we will live and do this or that." Otherwise you are

boasting about your own pretentious plans, and all
such boasting is evil (James 4:13–16).

When you know that your tomorrows are in God's hands, you become secure. He knows everything, including the things you cannot see. He knows what your plans are, and He knows about the storms ahead. He will not guarantee a trouble-free life, but He will *keep you* in good times and bad. Just trust Him! Defer to His will. Remind yourself that He is always good and trustworthy. Wrap yourself in Him, because *He* is your security. When uncertainty swirls all around you, the Rock of Ages will not be moved. Anchor yourself in Him!

No test or temptation that comes your way is beyond the
course of what others have had to face. All you need to
remember is that God will never let you down; he'll never
let you be pushed past your limit; he'll always be there
to help you come through it (1 Corinthians 10:13 MSG).

Bye, Bye Stuck Place

If anybody knew about stuck places, King David did. He endured the sorrows of shattered plans, betrayal, and heart-break. He experienced self-pity, grief, and feelings of insecurity. Yet he kept going and kept loving God. In my opinion, he is the best earthly example of encouraging yourself when all hope seems lost. I believe that part of his strength came from his willingness to share his true feelings with God. David did not hide his anger, frustration, and thoughts of revenge. The psalms he wrote are poignant because they are transparent and unabashedly human. Psalm 42 is all of that and shows just how David came to grips with adversity. Notice how diligently he tried to sort himself out before God:

> *Why am I so overwrought? Why am I so disturbed? Why can't I just hope in God? Despite all my emotions, I will believe and raise the One who saves me and is my life. My God, my soul is so traumatized; the only help is remembering You wherever I may be (Psalms 42:5–6 VOICE).*

David was real with himself and with God. He recognized his moments of imbalance and asked, "Why am I so worked up? What in the world is stressing me out? Why can't I just trust God?" He owned his heartache and articulated his anguish. He even admitted that his soul was traumatized! It took maturity of character to process his feelings this way. Even in his distress he seemed determined to break his emotional spiral and avoid a total meltdown. He did not try to prove how strong he was; he simply encouraged himself and cried out to God!

This is how David learned to move himself out of the dark places and into the light. Many of his psalms model this process, as Psalm 27 does:

> *The LORD is my light and my salvation—so why should I be afraid? The LORD is my fortress, protecting me from danger, so why should I tremble? When evil people come to devour me, when my enemies and foes attack me, they will stumble and fall. Though a mighty army surrounds me, my heart will not be afraid. Even if I am attacked, I will remain confident (Psalms 27: 1–3).*

Notice that David did not deny his fears and disappointments; he took them to God and worked through them.

That's self-discipline! He was willing to learn from his sorrows and govern himself. Because he processed his self-pity, grief, and insecurity, he accomplished great things in spite of them. He vented in God's presence but moved on. Instead of pouting, accusing, blaming, justifying himself, and whining to others, David got out of his ditch and found his security and healing in God.

With God's help, he got unstuck!

Freedom in Adversity

To get unstuck is to find freedom in the midst of your adversity. That is what David's life shows us. He experienced dark seasons, but he always turned to God and found hope again. In Psalms 27:13 he wrote, "I will move past my enemies with this one, sure hope: that with my own eyes, I will see the goodness of the Eternal in the land of the living" (VOICE). David had the same hope we have or can have: he expected to see God's goodness, not just in heaven but in this life. This expectation pulled him past his enemies and out of self-pity, grief, insecurity, and all kinds of misery.

David clung to another promise: "He makes me whole again, steering me off worn, hard paths to roads where truth and righteousness echo His name" (Ps. 23:3 VOICE). This is the very thing we seek: for God to make us whole again, steering us away from the hard, fruitless paths and toward paths of truth and righteousness, where His goodness frees us and bring Him glory. When we walk in this promise, we can face our adversity without fear and march straight through it, knowing that God is with us. We cry out to Him just like David did. Our seasons of disorientation and despair are no different from his. He lived through the very emotions we are living through now, thousands of years later. And he wrote about them for our sakes.

Even more important than what David did is what Jesus did: He suffered and *died* for our sakes. He took on human flesh and fully identified with us so that we could identify with Him. No one sees and understands our pain better than He does! He endured the greatest trial of all and suffered what none of us will ever suffer. He walked through the gates of hell for our sakes and rose from the dead. At this very moment, He knows what each of us is going through, and He has made provision to meet every need.

Yes—Jesus understands everything *you* are going through! He is not standing idly by but interceding for you, even now (Heb. 7:25). He will help you to process your adversity and grow from it. He knows what your preferences and frustrations are. He understands how perplexed you become when He doesn't intervene in the ways or timing you expect. He knows how much it hurts when nothing seems to be working and you feel "stalled out."

Jesus also knows that your stuck place is not a life sentence. He is already working in your situation. Invite Him into your struggle. Tell Him when you feel stranded or even forsaken. Admit that you feel afraid. Let go of what you thought was supposed to happen. He knows how much you invested in that other outcome. He understands how hard it is to move on. But if you will trust Him, He will lift you above the fray and carry you across your "junkyard." Let Him re-form and reshape your hope and use every part of your journey—especially the hardest parts!

Dear friend, your adversity is real. Yet God is much bigger than anything that would try to take you down. Keep your eyes on Him. Keep learning to see as He sees. Then move on with Him and follow wherever He leads. *He will not leave you.* He will see you through every challenge, and He will mend your broken places.

He really is *that* good!

LIVE AND LEARN

- Have you ever visited the stuck place? Are you there now? What does that look like for you? What is it costing you, and what has been the hardest part of getting out?

- Are you entertaining self-pity, or are you tempted to do so? What triggers feelings of self-pity in your life? What seeming comfort does your self-pity offer? Is it really a benefit? Why or why not?

- Is grief or insecurity keeping you stuck? How might you work through it and allow God and trusted friends to help you find more clarity? What have you learned about your most recent stuck place, and how can it help you to avoid stuck places in the future?

Afterword: Victory!

———✦———

As you read these words, you might be in the throes of
adversity and thankful that, in Christ, you have the victory. What a great consolation that is—especially when you are
pressed on every side and feel as though you have one hand tied
behind your back. When you come to the rock-solid realization
that your circumstances cannot doom you and God will never
forget you, you are on shouting ground! Even if everyone else
has given you up for lost, you can rest assured that God will
have the last word.

It is absolutely true: if you are in Christ, victory is assured.
He has made every provision for you to triumph. To seal your
fate, He laid down His life, spilled His blood, rose from the
dead, and returned to the Father's right hand. In doing so, He
guaranteed victory to everyone who would receive His gift and
worship Him. If you are one of them, you cannot help but win.

There is a catch, however. It is not a trick or a test of worthiness. Nor is it a secret code or stipulation that plays sleight
of hand with the cross of Christ. What He promised, He promised. And what He purchased through Calvary, He purchased.
It is finished. The price of your victory has been paid in full.
Therefore, the "catch" has nothing to do with Him but everything to do with you! It is a matter of understanding not only
what victory is, but what it isn't.

That is the catch! We tend to see victory as the absence of
struggles. We feel victorious when we win, but we see ourselves
as losers when we suffer. The beginning words of this book

summed it up, saying, "Of all the things we hope to avoid, resist, or remove, adversity tops the list." Nobody wants to suffer. The mere thought of adversity makes us uncomfortable. Yet we live in a fallen world where the absence of struggle is not an option.

Jesus said we would "have many trials and sorrows" but instructed us to "take heart" because He has "overcome the world" (John 16:33). He was letting us know that no matter what happens, our victory is assured. It might not be our idea of victory, but it is victory in the greatest sense of the word.

Obviously, Jesus doesn't see victory the way we see it. But guess who's right! His victory—the greatest and most consequential triumph in all of history—did not come by *avoiding* the cross or overcoming those who crucified Him. His victory came *through* the cross. Therefore, our victory does not come by overpowering our adversity or "just making it stop." That is not how we win. We are victorious when we walk through our adversity in ways that glorify Him and testify to everyone around us that, because of Jesus, our trouble does not overcome us. Adversity might cost us something, but it does not destroy us. Why? Because Christ in us is the very hope of glory (Col. 1:27).

If you are in the thick of trouble this very moment, know this: your trial is not a sign of failure, and your victory doesn't come when your trial ends. Your victory happens *in* the struggle. It comes when you find yourself in the junkyard, but the junkyard can't find itself in you. You win when His light shines through you in your darkest days. You are a victor when you point to Christ in the midst of your suffering.

That, my friend, is *victory*—pure, simple, and eternal.

ENDNOTES

1   Barna Research, "Most American Christians Do Not Believe That Satan or the Holy Spirit Exist," barna.com, April 13, 2009, https://www.barna.com/research/most-american-christians-do-not-believe-that-satan-or-the-holy-spirit-exist/.

2   *Dictionary.com*, s.v. "courage," accessed March 4, 2021, https://www.dictionary.com/browse/courage?s=t.

3   The prefix *dis* negates whatever follows it. The most basic meaning of *discouragement* is "not courage."

4   *Dictionary.com*, s.v. "courage," accessed March 4, 2021, https://www.dictionary.com/browse/courage?s=t.

5   *PTL Counsellors Edition Bible,* Holy Bible King James Edition (Fort Mill, SC: PTL Television, 1975), s.v. "Matthew 18:24."

6   Wordnik.com, s.v. "certainty," accessed March 24, 2021, https://www.wordnik.com/words/certain.

7   Perry R. Branson, "Shame: A Third Pillar of Civilization," *Psychology Today*, March 30, 2011, https://www.psychologytoday.com/us/blog/shrinkwrapped/201103/shame-third-pillar-civilization.

8   Jeff VanVonderen, *Families Where Grace Is in Place: Building a Home Free of Manipulation, Legalism, and Shame* (Minneapolis: Bethany House, 2010), 31; italics mine.

9   *Merriam-Webster Online Dictionary*, s.v. "validate," accessed March 23, 2021, https://www.merriam-webster.com/dictionary/validate.

10 *The American Heritage Dictionary*, s.v. "pity," accessed April 27, 2021, https://ahdictionary.com/word/search.html?q=pity.